Martial Arts, Self-Defense and a Whole Lot More: The Best of Wim's Blog

Volume 1

by
Wim Demeere

Also by Wim Demeere:

Books:
The Fighter's Guide to Hard-Core Heavy Bag Training
Timing in the Fighting Arts
The Fighter's Body

Videos:
Combat Sanshou: The Punishing Chinese Fighting Art, Part One: Striking
Combat Sanshou: The Punishing Chinese Fighting Art, Part Two: Kicking
Combat Sanshou: The Punishing Chinese Fighting Art, Part Three: Takedowns, Throws, and Finishing Moves
The Fighter's Video Guide to Hard-Core Heavy Bag Training
Pad Man, A Video Guide to Full-Contact Partner Training

For an up to date page with direct links to all these books and videos, please go here:
www.wimsblog.com/products

Dedication

To Lauren and Xander.
You light up my life like nobody else can.
There are no words for how much I love you both.

Contents

Introduction

Some things you need to know before you start reading:

First off, the vast majority of these posts come from my blog, which you can find at www.wimsblog.com. I'm a reasonably active blogger so feel free to drop on by and read all the other content I have there.

Second, I had to edit the posts so they make sense in book format. Meaning, I cut out all the direct links to websites because, well, I guess you can always *try* to make this book go on-line... Instead of giving you direct links, I wrote "Do an internet search on..." followed by a specific term or keywords. This way, you'll be able to quickly find what I'm talking about.

Sometimes I refer directly to blog posts, mentioning the title. The same thing applies here: go to www.wimsblog.com and use the search function to find the relevant post to read the information I'm referring to.

Finally, I also cut up posts, re-named and re-structured them or deleted paragraphs to make it all work in both e-book format and in print. These formats are very different from a blog and need that type of tweaking. But you can always find the original information by going to my blog and typing in the title of the post in the search function.

I think this version here is better because I've had more time to edit the content. When I post on my blog, it is all still very fresh in my mind which sometimes means it doesn't come out exactly right. So hopefully the time that passed between writing the original posts and editing this book has helped me clarify everything and has improved the writing.

When I mention names, most of them refer to people who commented on the blog posts. If you want to know more about them, again, go to my blog and use the search function to find the relevant posts and comments.

You'll see one of the main themes in my writing come through pretty quickly:

The differences are just as important as the similarities.

I found this to be a life-changing concept. It put me on the path of finding more information, better training, exploring different arts, and much more. But what is even more important: it helped me learn and progress much, much faster than I otherwise would have. You'll mostly see this theme when I write about MMA as compared to other arts and as a result you might get the impression that I'm against MMA. I'm not, not in the least. I think it's an awesome sport and to compete in it you need big balls of steel combined with supreme athletic abilities. If I were 18 right now, that's what I'd want to compete in.

That said, lots of people don't seem to want nuanced discussion anymore. They want things to be black or white:

"MMA sucks!"
"MMA is the best!"

Neither one of these statements is 100% correct or false. The same goes for lots of other topics of discussion. Which brings me to another point I think is crucial:

There can be more than one right answer.

Even though we might disagree with each other, we can still both be right. It all depends on our definitions of the terms we use, context and so on. So for me to be right, you don't necessarily have to be wrong and vice versa. But for that to work, we both have to be on the same page about how to discuss or argue. The way I like to do that is this:

The value of a discussion lies not in proving you are right and the other person is wrong; it lies in *the exchange of ideas*. It lies in re-evaluating your own and your opponent's position, regardless of the conclusions you come to afterwards.

It's with all this in mind that I write on my blog and also how I wrote this book. It doesn't really matter if you agree with me or not. What matters is that we both think about our arguments pro and con, and then hopefully gain some new insights.

I did my best to achieve that goal in this book.

I hope you enjoy the read.

Wim Demeere

How to piss off your training partner

I first wanted to name this guide "How to Piss Off your Training Partner and Get Your Butt Whipped" but figured that might be a bit excessive… Not everything in my top three list will get you beat up in class, so some moderation is in order. But the behaviour I'll describe often results in the offender getting either a beating, a couple of nasty blows under the radar or at the very least the training partner doesn't want to play anymore.

What I'm talking about? Annoying the crap out of your training partner. Doing things that piss him off because he doesn't get to train correctly or you do something dangerous, something that can cause him injury.

Over the years, I've experienced a lot of situations in which I wanted to tear my partner's head off. Sometimes I was forced to get rough on that partner to make him stop. Other times, I only had to point out what he was doing and ask him to stop. There were also instances where I lost my cool and had to restrain myself from doing damage. We're all human and nobody has endless patience. Other times, you just don't have a choice.

To place this in proper context: there are a couple of reasons why training partners might piss you off and it isn't always clear which one it is:

- **Communication failure.** Your partner misunderstood the teacher and does something different from what you heard. Or he misunderstood what you said. This happens a lot and is often the first reason why things go wrong.
- **Ego.** We all have an ego and it's easy to get emotionally hijacked by it: "How dare that white belt/beginner land such a solid punch on my handsome face! Doesn't he know I'm a black belt and

God's gift to mankind?!" That's when you throw your next punch a little too fast and hard… Or the flip side of that coin: "OMG, I hope nobody saw that he got me good… Everybody will laugh and think I suck. I better show them I can stomp this idiot into the ground." Nobody likes to lose face in front of his peers.

- **Mismatched assumptions.** This one has many aspects to it but the common thread is each practitioner has a different idea about something and assumes the other is on the same page. For instance, if you know certain techniques your partner doesn't, assuming he knows how to defend against the ones he hasn't learned yet is a recipe for disaster. It's also something you can easily overlook.

- **Physical attributes.** The teacher says to practice at half-speed or half-strength. But that doesn't mean the same thing to everybody: If your top speed for punching is 100Mph, half of that is 50Mph. If your partner maxes out at 60Mph, he'll expect you to come at him at 30Mph and isn't ready for what you throw. Then he gets pissed because he thinks you're out to hurt him. And then you get pissed because you don't see what you did wrong and why he's getting all uppity.

- **Training methods**. Some practitioners like to train rough and tumble, others prefer to take things slow and ingrain the technique first before increasing speed and power. A mismatch between these training methods leads to two pissed off people in no time.

- **Liberties vs. cooperation.** Some students assume they have to resist their partner when he practices his joint locks on them; if he can't make it work against a resisting opponent, they feel he's not it right. Others think you have to get the mechanics down first and then gradually increase the difficulty by adding resistance. Or your partner feels he can just hit you whenever you leave yourself unprotected when you perform a technique. Sometimes, you're allowed to get creative as you train, other times you have to stay within specific guidelines and cooperate with your partner. If you are both on a different page, it'll get interesting real fast.

- **Ignorance, viciousness and stupidity.** Sometimes people are just plain stupid or mean. They do idiotic things like throwing a sharpened throwing star at you to see if you catch it (I deflected it but still got cut). Or they suddenly punch high when you're supposed to be practicing a defense against a low punch, just to see if they can get you (I slapped his fist away, grabbed him by the throat and almost slammed him head-first onto the floor before I realized he was just being an asshole.) And the list goes on and on ad nauseam.

We'll look at what you can do about this in the next part. But for now, here are the top three things that piss me off when I'm training:

1) *I'm bigger than him so he feels he can hit me harder than I can hit him.*

This one, I still don't get after several decades of training. Just because I'm a heavyweight, doesn't mean I'm your punching bag. This should be common sense but in my experience, it isn't. Just because I can take heavier impacts than a lighter opponent, doesn't mean that I *have* to. If the shot is hard enough, it still hurts regardless of how much my partner weighs. I've had this happen so many times, I don't believe it's coincidence. It's a total lack of respect that can get the lighter guy in over his head, especially if he has misconceptions about heavyweights (like that we're all slow...)

Think of it like poking a tiger with a stick and then complaining that you get ripped up because that big cat is stronger and heavier than you. Newsflash! Don't poke the tiger and you don't get hurt! Play nice! And if he does claw you to pieces, well then you only have yourself to blame: it's not like you didn't know he was heavier and stronger than you when you decided it would be fun to mess with him.

2) *They hit where you're going, not where you are.*

Some people just don't get the process of training. E.g.: you practice dodging a punch to the left and they turn their punch into a heat seeking missile: it goes straight to where your head will be when you finish dodging. Of course you get nailed! How could you not? It's the martial arts version of predicting the future: it only works when you cheat. Meaning, your partner *knows upfront* you'll dodge to the left. So it doesn't take a rocket scientist to time his punch to where your head is going in such a way that you can't do anything about it.

It's beyond me why people do this. Like taking candy from a baby; any idiot can do it. But strangely enough, when I return the favour, these same guys complain. Hey buddy, if you don't want to stay within the parameters of the drill, why should I?

3) *They block the technique(s) you're supposed to be learning.*

One time at a seminar, I almost put a guy through the window because he kept doing just that: we were practicing knife defense by redirecting a thrust and then striking back a few times. Each time I did those counters, he blocked them or parried and cut me again. Great, another genius… Of course you can do that when you know *exactly* what I'll be doing next and *when* I'll do it. It doesn't get more obvious than this. But in the mean time, I'm not training the technique at all. So what's in it for me then? He gets to stroke his ego and thinks he's hot stuff because he blocked everything I dealt out; I learn nothing. Worse, in reality he's not learning anything either because he's predicting the future like I explained in the previous bullet. So it's just a big waste of time.

In Part Two, I'll cover some more annoying crap people pull and offer some suggestions on how to handle this.

How to piss off your training partner, Part 2

In part one of this guide, I mentioned my top-three annoyances when training with another practitioner. In this part here, we'll look at some other gripes I have. Given the feedback (I asked for and received in spades) they seem to be pretty universal. So here goes another round of ranting, continuing the list from part one:

4) **Endless counters.** Bert mentioned this in the comments section and it ties in with #3 *"They block the technique(s) you're supposed to be learning."* But this time they go about it in a sneakier way. Instead of flat out resisting, they drag you into an endless counter series "If you do that punch, I can block like this. And if you then kick me, I'll evade like this". And it goes on and on. The reality these guys fail to see is that *every technique has at least* one *counter.* So of course you can always do something about it in theory.

In reality, there's only so much time to do the counter they have in mind: time is measured in milliseconds in a fight. By the time they figure out how counter your attack, you could have hit him several times already. That's how it works in real life, but of course they prefer their dojo-fantasy.

On top of that, they're predicting the future again, as mentioned before. It's easy to counter what I do when they know *upfront* which technique I'll use. But when I can pick my techniques at random, I land them every time against these guys. And then they don't understand why their counter doesn't work. Shees…

5) **"This doesn't work."** This is such a classic, it feels redundant but I'll mention it anyway. Imagine you're trying a new technique on a partner and he starts the dance by saying your technique won't work on him. Obviously, he can back this up because *he knows exactly what you'll be doing* (There's a theme here…) The flaw in his reasoning isn't clear to Mr. Genius: you'd have to be a poor schmuck if you can't

mess up your partner's technique when you have advance warning of what he'll do. There's nothing to it; anybody can pull that off. Take away the advance warning and then see what happens to our rocket scientist… Pfff…

6) **"We do this too, but better."** This one was also brought up in the comments and is another pet peeve of mine. It's when you work with somebody who's new but already has some training. Or when you train at another school and they want to show you they are just sooooo much better than you. Or when you're at a seminar with people from lots of different systems and their ego needs to know they're top-dog. Basically, whatever you are practicing, your partner tells you he already knows it and then proceeds to show you other stuff. The worst offenders are usually those who have real crappy skills. They think they know it already but are so far from it, it's pointless to explain it to them.

I once taught a seminar about basic combinations and how to use them with good tactics. There was a teacher who participated and when I asked him if he was having fun, he said it was too basic and he already knew these combinations. I didn't have the heart to tell him how wrong he was. He was competent alright but he couldn't get the timing and flow of the combinations to work, it wasn't even close. Because of that, he didn't get the results we were training for. He made the classic mistake of seeing only the similarities he already knew instead of the differences I was showing him.

Yup, he already knew it all. But then why was it he got scored on all the time and had no defense against my students who *did* do what I showed them?

7) **"I don't want to hurt you honey."** Restita brought up an interesting perspective: male-female interactions. A lot of guys don't know how to train with women or girls. They're often way too soft, refusing to attack with at least a minimum of speed and power. I even had a student refuse to train with a young lady because "He didn't hit women." I told her to have fun and smack him around as hard as she wanted. She did and he changed his mind after a while (of course, I monitored what was going on both during and after the smack-fest.)

"Female" doesn't automatically mean "weak". If you think it does, you haven't met enough women… Besides, it's a matter of respect to your training partner; give her at least enough to work with so she can train in a realistic manner. She won't be attacked by overly gentle opponents in the street so don't act like one in class.

Another aspect to this is macho/asshole behaviour towards female students. Like Restita said: calling her "babe" or honey", probably with an arrogant smirk on his face. What's up with that? I even prefer my student's over-chivalrous reaction to this kind of stupidity. A minimum of respect between partners isn't too much to ask for.

8) **"I don't want to you to think you suck, honey."** Frederick made an excellent remark: some students go to the opposite extreme of denigrating a female student by pretending everything they do works great, even (or especially) when it's clear to everybody she's doing it wrong. It's denigrating to women and a double standard to the men in the class. Sure, there is a learning curve for everybody; you can't expect students to pull off a technique right away and sometimes you have to give them a self-esteem boost by letting them "win". But over-acting doesn't help women either. They need honest feedback to know if their technique works or not. Acting in an "I better drop as soon as she touches me because she's a girl" way doesn't help anybody. And it's sexist to boot.

9) **Work on another technique than the one shown.** In all fairness, this sometimes happens without doing it on purpose. Especially if you've been training for a while, you tend to default into certain techniques when the intensity goes up. But some people do this deliberately: the teacher shows a technique and they proceed to do something else. In the mean time, you don't get to study what the teacher showed you because Mr. Nice Guy decides he wants to do other stuff. How much more difficult does it get: Teacher says, students does. Period. Mr. Myagi had it right…

10) **150Mph baby!! YIHAAAH!!!!** This is for all the studs and jocks out there. Let me put it clearly: You don't learn a new technique by always doing it as hard and as fast as you can. You don't even train this way with techniques you've been doing for years. Yes, there is place

for hardcore training and personally, I love it. But that isn't the only way to train or even the most efficient. Not by a long shot.

There's tons of value in practicing at a lower intensity, especially when you're learning something new or your partner just isn't as fast/strong as you. Especially if the latter is true, you learn *absolutely nothing* by cranking it up. You already know you can beat your partner and he obviously can't match that intensity. So what's the upside for you or your partner? Besides wagging your pecker in front of him to show him just how big it is? Wow, you manly-man you!

Once again, say it with me and with feeling: pffff….

That's it for Part Two. It turned out a bit longer than expected thanks to all the great comments. In part three, I'll focus on how to deal with this shitty behaviour.

How to piss off your training partner, Part 3

In part one and two of this guide, we looked at several things your training partners do to piss you off. Perhaps they do it on purpose, perhaps not, but you'll have to deal with it one way or the other. So what can you do?

A bunch of things actually and not all of them work with everybody. Sometimes you have to mix and match, other times nothing works and you skip to the bottom of this list of suggestions:

- **Communication.** You need to figure out a way to explain to your partnerwhy he's pissing you off. And you'll have to stay calm too or the situation can escalate. Easier said than done with some people but this is the most polite way to settle the problem. Some ideas:

  - Just tell him in the calmest possible way what is upsetting you. Be precise and concise; don't start into a long, winding speech. Then ask him not to do that anymore. Say please and be as polite as you can be.
  - Humour can defuse a lot of situations. Make fun of it but try to get your message across. My personal favourite for guys who crank it up too much: "Dude! I'm an over-the-hill, brittle, old fart. Stop hitting me so hard, man. Otherwise I might break and I left my wheelchair at home!"
  - Involve the teacher. Instead of arguing with your partner, just say you think you're supposed to work on another technique than what he's doing or you should practice it in another way. Before he can reply, tell him you'll ask the teacher and simultaneously start walking away.

- **Demonstrate.** Show the partner what he's doing. He might not realize he's messing up and getting on your nerves. You could say: "Hey, we're supposed to work on a wrist lock, not an elbow lock.

13

Can we get back to what the teacher showed?" In other gyms and schools the same thing might be said like this "Hey man, you're doing a frikkin' elbow lock again. It's supposed to be a wrist lock, dumbass. Get with the program!" Of course, there is a lot of middle ground between both extremes here. You decide which way to go, it's your face…

- **Call him on it.** This takes it up a notch and could get you into trouble. But it's something a certain type of training partner gets real well. I think it was John who gave a good example, here's what he said:

*Seriously though, every time I learned a joint lock, the idea was that I should generally do something to distract them first and then apply the lock. While I understand that this is *practice* and you shouldn't have to do that while learning, I've found an incredulous "Is _that_ really how you want to do this?" question, followed up if necessary by softening them up just a bit, lets them understand that YES this technique could work in a fight, just not in the unrealistic you-stand-there-while-I-make-a-pretzel-out-of-you manner learning and practice sometimes require.*

This is the equivalent of giving a final warning. By calling your partner on his behaviour, especially if he's doing it intentionally, you let him know playtime is over. He now knows you'll do unto him as he did to you. If he still doesn't get it, then you move on to the next bullet.

- **Reciprocate.** Some people won't get it at all, even if you draw pictures. Then you have to do to them as they do to you. Just today, I taught a class to a bunch of young guys. In the end, they wanted to do something fun and I let them try to wrestle me on one small judo mat. If they could make me put one foot outside of it, they won. The rules were: no striking and no dirty stuff. Three of those guys started clawing with their fingernails to make me move. I told them to stop clawing or I'd return the favour. That didn't work so I grabbed some skin and twisted it around. Two of them let go and didn't do it again. One guy let go and then resumed his clawing. I responded in kind. He stopped but tried one more time. I told him I could rip him up harder than he could and dug in a bit more than before. He yelped in pain and then left it at that. Some people, out of malice or ignorance, have to learn the hard way.

- **Let it go and walk away.** This is arguable the hardest part. Especially if the partner pulled crap on you before, you feel entitled to give him a piece of your mind or make him suffer a bit. We've probably all been there. But if you can hold back your temper just a bit, think long term: What do you gain from letting the conflict escalate? Nine out of ten, it won't be worth it. Just bow out, step away and change partners.

Whatever you do, remember that he'll be back again next class. If you choose to get all bent out of shape and bust him up, odds are he'll try to return the favour then. If you make a fool out of him, you might have made an enemy. Or you might open his eyes and get a friend out of it, who knows?

One of my best friends was the guy I'd fight tooth and nail in class. We didn't like each other at all and played for keeps. After bashing each other's skull in a few times throughout the years, our attitudes changed and we became brothers in arms. So everything is possible.

How to avoid shoulder injuries in the martial arts.

Shoulder injuries are some of the most common injuries in the martial arts. If you've been training for a while, chances are high you've faced them before. Unfortunately, so have I. Case in point:

One of the wrestling drills I do in my Sanshou class is "King of the hill". The concept is very simple and many teachers use it:

- Two students face off and try to throw, sweep or trip each other.
- The first one to fall (or the one at the bottom if both fall) leaves the mat and is replaced by the next student.
- The goal is to stay on the mat as long as possible, fighting fresh opponents every single time.

We do this drill regularly at the end of class as it's always fun. It also really wipes you out if you can stay "king" for a while. Even if you don't, it's still good training: before it's your turn again, you get enough rest to *really* go at it.

Last week, we did the drill again, everything went fine and we had a blast. I went home after class, watched some TV to wind down and when I got up, my shoulder ached. I figured, no big deal, been there before. But the next morning, I ached a lot more; I'd lost some mobility and gained some pain whenever I lifted my arm. At that point I went "Damn, again..." and started assessing the damage before beginning a rehab program. My shoulder's better now but I'm still doing the exercises to make sure there's no lasting damage and I can train at 100% again as soon as possible.

What causes shoulder injuries?

The list of potential causes is long but here are the usual suspects:

- **Overdoing it.** In our martial arts training, we punch, kick and grapple hard all the time. This puts tremendous stress on your shoulders and if you don't build in enough recuperation between training sessions, your body becomes prone to injury. When your shoulders are over-fatigued, even a light movement or small technical mistake can cause a tear or sprain. It doesn't mean you're weak, it only means your body is tired and (like it or not) it's telling you to take some rest.
- **Too many reps.** You can overdo it by training too hard for too long and with not enough rest as I explained in the previous bullet. But you can also do too many repetitions of the same movement, class after class, wearing your muscles down. Until suddenly, your shoulders can't take it anymore.
- **Violent shock.** Your shoulder is a relatively weak joint because of its "ball and socket" structure. If you receive a sudden, violent shock to it and you aren't tightening up the shoulder along with its surrounding muscles, you can easily injure it. Ask anybody who's had a shoulder lock slammed on him when he didn't expect it. Ouch…

There are more causes for shoulder problems than this but for the average martial artist, these are the most common ones.
The biggest issue with shoulder injuries is this: *it's very hard to let them heal completely.*

You need your arms in almost every activity you do. This makes it difficult to get enough rest and have the problem go away by healing completely. As a result, too many martial artists and fighters make the mistake of training too hard, too soon. They then create a chronic injury out of one that could have gone away had they waited a little bit longer.

What are the symptoms of a shoulder injury?

So how do you know you messed up your shoulder by resisting that omoplata during BJJ class? Here are a couple tell-tale signs:
- **Pain.** I can hear the cries of "Well, duh!" already but it is the

clearest indicator something's wrong. Dull pain, sharp pain, it's all bad.

- **Decreased range of motion.** This is another no-brainer: if you suddenly can't move your shoulder through full range of motion anymore, something is wrong.

- **All of the above.** Sometimes you'll have no pain at all, except when you lift or turn your arms in a specific way. Or you might feel light pain all over but it suddenly hurts much more when you move your arm in one direction and then can't go any further. Either way, your shoulder is messed up.

- **No feeling.** If you don't feel anything anymore in your shoulder or arm, you're on your way to FUBAR City. Seek medical help *right away*.

Again, there's more to it than this but these are good rules of thumb.

What do I do now?

Well, it's your life so feel free to do whatever you want. Me? I've had shoulder problems that took six months to heal because I didn't treat them correctly. So now, I take them seriously. Here's what I do these days:

- **When it hurts a LOT right away.** Whenever I feel something snap or it hurts like the blazes and doesn't go away in a few minutes, I'm off to the hospital. In my experience, that means something bad happened and I need to get control of it right away. If I don't, it usually gets worse the longer I wait to get a doctor to look at it.

- **When it hurts a lot but the pain goes away after a few minutes.** I take it slow for the remainder of my training session. If I was punching on the heavy bag, I switch to kickingso I can finish my work out. After a while, I'll throw some light punches to seeif everything is still working correctly and to check for pain. If the pain doesn't go away completely, I'm off to the hospital the next day.

- **If it doesn't hurt during training but suddenly it does when I**

get home or the day after. I do what happened to me last week: I check the range of motion, asses the pain and then slowly do stretching and strengthening exercises. To avoid making the injury worse, I stay well away from the pain threshold.

That's how I handle shoulder injuries these days. I don't get them as much as before, mainly because I work on prevention a lot more now. But as last week's class demonstrated, you're never immune to them.

One caveat: *when in doubt, seek medical help.* This is what works for me and I only learned it after a lot of trial and error. But things might be different for you so don't hesitate to seek medical help whenever you're in doubt.

How to avoid shoulder injuries in the martial arts, Part Two

In part one of this guide, I talked about my personal experience with shoulder injuries and how I deal with them today. In this part we'll look at how to prevent them. But before we do that, allow me to make a simple yet important point:

Prevention only works if you make a long-term commitment to it.

I've been a personal trainer for 18 years now and have taught all sorts of clients: young and old, men and women, out of shape and in peak condition, healthy 60-year olds and people recovering from their second heart attack at age 27. Regardless of these factors, there is only *one* that really matters in my experience: commitment. The clients who committed to their goals eventually reached them. Those who started training and were in it for the long term are still working out today. Some of the clients I've had from day one are still training with me after 18 years of working together.

That's the kind of commitment I'm talking about.

So if you want to prevent shoulder problems, you have to view training for that goal as a *long term plan and integrate it into your training schedule.* If you only do it sporadically, you'll get mediocre results at best.

The biggest psychological mistake people make is this: They think they'll *always* have to work as hard as when they start such a prevention program. That's simply not true. When you start on a prevention program, you do have to take out sufficient time for it, that's true. But it won't keep absorbing that amount of time forever. In most cases, you can get good results with only 10-15min. of work every other day. Once you get the desired results, you go into maintenance mode and reduce the sessions to twice a week. Or you could incorporate them into your regular training (especially the stretching part). Then a month or two later, you increase the sessions again, back to three times a week if you feel your shoulders need it. Experiment and see what works best for you but do make it a part of your overall training.

The two pillars of prevention.

To have healthy shoulders, you need two things: *strength training* and *stretching*. Your shoulders have to become both strong *and* flexible at the same time. Just one or the other doesn't cut it. You need both for martial arts and combat sports:

- **If you're flexible but not strong,** you can easily injure your shoulders by placing them in an extreme position and then lacking the strength to resist a load bearing down on them. That happens for instance when you resist a shoulder lock when your shoulder is already stretched to the limit. Or you might throw a sloppy punch that places the shoulder in a weak position and your muscles aren't strong enough to handle the impact.
- **If you're strong but not flexible**, your muscles can end up so tensed up they actually cause you pain and discomfort when you train. This usually happens when you don't stretch them enough. Or when you use too much strength in every move you do, constantly locking up your shoulder muscles, which results in an even greater loss of flexibility. Then you move your arm in a larger range of motion and something snaps because it isn't flexible enough.

A good prevention program works on both these aspects; strength *and* flexibility.

Here are some of the things I like to do and have been doing for the last few weeks since my injury

Strength training

Your two main targets are the shoulder muscle and the rotator cuff. First, the shoulder muscle (deltoid):

- The basic exercises are the shoulder press, lateral raise, front raise and bent-over lateral raise. Just do a search for these on the internet and you'll find tons of articles and videos on how to do them correctly.
- Don't go for the bodybuilding-style training with these exercises because that's not what you need. Your goal isn't to build huge amounts of muscle mass but to strengthen the shoulder.
- Take it slow; don't go for heavy weights and loads of sets/reps right from the start. Again, you don't need huge shoulders to strengthen them for your MMA or karate practice. It's nice to have such shoulders and women might like it (yeah, I know you were thinking about just that...) but stay focused on the goal: strengthening your shoulders to avoid injuries.
- Focus on good technique instead of how much you lift or how many reps/sets you do. If you want to play it safe, get professional instruction to make sure you do the exercises right.

Next, the rotator cuff:

- Instead of focusing on specific exercises, focus on the function of the rotator cuff: abduction of the arm, internal rotation and external rotation.
- Do an internet search for "rotator cuff exercises" and you'll find just how many there are. Failing that, ask a physical therapist for some suggestions.
- Go easy and do smooth movements. The goal is not to work on explosiveness but to stabilize and strengthen your shoulders.
- Pain means you have to stop. You do **not** want to tear your rotator cuff muscles, believe me as I speak from bitter experience here. So don't train them with the "No pain, no gain" mind set.
- The most important piece of advice is this: *don't neglect the rotator cuff*. If your shoulder muscles (deltoids) are strong, the rotator cuffs need to be strong too as they act as stabilizers. So add these exercises to your routine, even if you don't like them because they aren't cool and don't add muscle to your frame. Again, it's not about impressing the ladies...

One word of caution: if you have a shoulder injury, go see an MD first, before trying any of these exercises. You don't want to experiment and make things worse.

Stretching

Martial artists and fighters stretch their lower body all the time but often only gloss over the upper body, especially the shoulders. Eventually, they lose flexibility and become prone to injuries. Stretching the shoulder (both the deltoid and rotator cuff) isn't all that hard to do though. The hardest thing is reminding yourself to actually do these stretches. Just give them a place in your daily stretching routine and then you won't forget them. A couple more pointers:

- Do an internet search for "rotator cuff stretches" or "rotator cuff stretching" to find a truckload of stretches you can do.
- Build it up slowly. If you haven't stretched your shoulders a lot, don't force it. As with all stretching, the key is to relax into it and not fight it. With new stretches, you have to learn that first for those specific muscles, before you can push it a bit.
- Do these stretches every time you do the strength training for your shoulder. Strength and flexibility should go hand-in-hand.

I know you can do a lot more exercises to make your shoulders more flexible but that's not the goal of this guide. The idea is to get you started right away, without having to learn some insanely difficult yoga posefirst.

Good luck!

How to learn techniques from video

I first wanted to title this post "How to learn fighting techniques form a video and avoid making a fool of yourself." but that's probably a bit too much. So I left out the last part but you know it's there in my mind...

I'll get to the "learning techniques" part in a bit but I want to cover something else first. Namely, this post is a case of several random things coming together:

- I first wrote something on this subject in a previous post.
- I just finished taping the introduction to the free-video lessons for the subscribers to my blog. In one of those videos, I comment on receiving negative reactions on YouTube.
- But what kicked if off was a rude reaction I got last week on one of my YouTube videos called "Tai Chi Chuan and Combat SanshouTechniques" which you can search for there.

As I said before, I'm used to getting silly, stupid and rude comments on my videos and that's fine. Somebody saying I can't fight my way out of a wet paper bag doesn't change my skills for the better or the worse. So why should I get upset about it?

However, when my teachers tell me I'm doing a terrible job, that's when I bang my head against the wall in both frustration and shame. After picking myself up from the floor, I do all I can to fix the problem they corrected me on. But some anonymous person on the Internet? To quote Stephen King: "Fughedaboutit!"

Anyway, "80KungFu" left the following comment on that video:

"What are you talking about? The man (Wim Demeere), clearly says, himself, that he is using Tai Chi techniques! Grasp the birds tail and single whip fucking

whip! Now I don't agree with his knowledge (mostly I think his Tai Chi skills and knowledge are terrible), but he stills says that he is using Tai Chi techniques! So what the fuck are you talking about?"

80KungFu actually deleted his comments after I sent him a mail explaining:

- I was talking about other comments, not his.
- I am sorry he doesn't like my skills all that much but look forward to his videos so we can compare notes.
- I am close to deleting his comment because even though I don't mind profanity, I don't want it on my YouTube page.
- I also thanked him for inspiring me to write this blog post.

It's sad to see he now deleted his comments but that's his choice. As it so happens, I copy/pasted them in the mail I sent him and still have the email notifications from YouTube, the ones with his comments in quotes…

Anyway, he replied to my mail:

- With an apology for his tone. Apparently a lot of people "try to fuck with him" and he thought I was one of them. (I most certainly am not; my girlfriend wouldn't approve.)
- He still thinks my tai chi skills suck because the applications don't look like the form.
- How the last technique (Single whip) wouldn't work in real life because the attacker wouldn't "let me do the arm bar."
- I don't understand what he said, brag about my tournament trophies and think I'm great for having them.

When you put it all together, it isn't much of an apology really, especially the last part. Though I admit I did have a good laugh when I read his mail. In the face of such bile and ignorance, it's hard to do anything else but see humour in the situation.

Here's the thing: it's pretty easy to pick on a video,regardless of what is shown or who's in it. Especially if your arguments depend on flawed knowledge and a truckload of assumptions about the guy showing his stuff. This is precisely the case with my friend here.

But the biggest issue is this: Loads of people seem to have no clue at all about how making a video *actually works*. It doesn't matter if you're filming a martial arts technique or showing a ballet move, there are certain structures and guidelines to follow. Which specific goals the presenter has with the video and how he shows the content has a direct impact on what you'll see on the screen.

Another thing 80KungFu doesn't seem to understand is related to this but also germane to how people view training in general: Bob Orlando nailed it when he said (paraphrasing):

Accept that all training is nothing but a simulation of reality. The operative word being "simulation".

A real-life attack is not the same thing as training for such an event. Training prepares you for something and by definition cannot be identical to the real thing. I thought that was obvious, but apparently, it isn't. Especially in the fighting arts, people seem to miss this point. Not so in other sports though: when was the last time you heard somebody claim line drills are useless for football because nobody plays football in a line like that? Well, duh!

Training is simulation. Simulation has benefits and drawbacks.

The main benefit is that you get to analyze and practice specific skills, techniques, concepts, etc. The drawback is that there are always one or (many) more elements missing from the equation. But just because these elements aren't there, that doesn't mean the drill or training exercise is useless.

That's where 80Kung Fu drops the ball: He compares apples with oranges.

Of course I know that "in real life" an attacker won't leave his arm out there. Of course I know he'll want to attack me again when he notices his first punch didn't land. That's hardly rocket science. But in that video, I'm also *not doing the technique like I would in real life:*

- I'm showing it so the camera picks it up in the best possible way.
- I'm not trying to beat up my partner.

That's it for the first part. In the second one, I'll go into the different types of videos and give some more details on those missing elements.

How to learn techniques from video, Part 2

In part one I mentioned how there are different kinds of videos. Let's look at that a bit closer now.

You can distinguish three broad categories of videos: *Live footage*, *demonstration*, and *instructional* videos. These three are all vastly different from each other and that's where the trouble starts: if you expect one and get the other, you think it sucks. If you believe instructional videos are "The Truth"™, then you'll think demonstrations are bullshit. If you truly believe the best way to fight is what you see in live footage (because it's "real" and everything else isn't), then you'll laugh at instructional videos.

I believe the following two sayings apply when you want to learn from a video:

- **Don't compare apples and oranges.** Know what kind of video you're looking at and evaluate it as such.
- **Don't throw out the baby with the bathwater.** Instead of focusing on what you perceive is bad, look at what is good, interesting and potentially useful for you.

Especially this last part is crucial.

I've been reviewing books and videos for a long time and I have only one goal with them: To find value in the book or video and determine who would benefit from it. Maybe the book didn't do much for me, but that doesn't automatically make it useless for you. I always try to write something positive in a review and only rarely fail to find it. It's a matter of separating the good from the bad and mediocre that may also be there.

It's the same thing with watching a video: If you want to learn from it, whatever that "it" may be, search for the positive. If you only want to validate and reinforce your own ideas, that's fine too. But then don't complain when you can't find any decent videos because you find they're all crap.

Back on track, let's talk about those three categories:

Live footage

This one's pretty simple at first view: Something happens and a camera gets it on tape. Live footage is usually, but not always:

- **Poorly filmed.** The action is often hard to see because the cameraman moves too much. Or it's CCTV images taken form high above, which isn't always the best angle to view a fight. Or the image isn't detailed enough to show you what is actually going on.
- **Chaotic.** There's no time to set everything up and make sure the action is filmed perfectly: The fighters don't stay in the shot, they move behind obstacles, spectators walk in front of the camera and so on. You rarely get to see everything perfectly.

Type in "real fight" at YouTube.com and you'll get to see a boatload of scuffles, fights and assaults. Some are nothing but wild brawls where as others are over after the first (pre-emptive) punch. Sometimes you see good techniques but more often, the only thing that comes out is wild haymakers. All of these videos show "real fights" but every fight is different. Here's the thing where most people make erroneous assumptions:

If you've only been exposed to the violence you see in one of these videos, you might not believe the other kinds exist.

As a result, any information you find that shows these other types of fights looks fake to you. You'd be wrong in thinking this tough. Given the limited experience you have with violence, this mistake is understandable and not your fault. But you're still wrong. The problem I often have is convincing people this is the case with them. Because in their experience, all violence happens a certain way and me saying it doesn't usually ends with a challenge: "Prove it!"

The problem is that I can't. Nobody can. If every time you fought, you used a punch to KO your opponent, then you'll rightly claim punches are the best way to knock a guy out in a real fight. Yet I, and many others, have used high kicking techniques in the street to achieve the same result. So to us, your refusal to accept high kicks as potentially devastating self defense techniques seems totally incomprehensible. Because our experience of using them is *just as real to us as your experience using only punches*. So who's right?

We all are.

Violence is too big a subject for any one person. Nobody leads such an adventurous life that they end up experiencing all the different kinds of violence there exist in the world. Which means there is more than one truth. And for you to be right, I'm not necessarily wrong; we can both be right at the same time.

Keep this in mind when you watch a live video. Make sure your personal experience doesn't filter out the positive information you might discover. Live footage of an incident shows one thing and one thing only: that particular incident. But not every fight will be like that. Some will be worse; others will be a walk in the park by comparison. And it can always go from one extreme to the other in a heartbeat.

If you base your fighting techniques on what you see in a video of one particular type of violence, *it won't prepare you for the other kinds of violence out there*.

Demonstration

I'll distinguish this category from instructional videos by its emphasis: It only shows things but *doesn't* explain them.

Stating the obvious, demonstration videos are meant to show something, usually in a positive way. There are some basic ways to go about it:

- **Crisp and clean.** Just showing the techniques and nothing else. You want to show *skill*.
- **Spectacular.** The same techniques, but emphasized and exaggerated to make them look more over the top. You want to *impress* people.
- **Dramatic.** Now we're moving into Hollywood territory by using camera angles, lighting, music/sound effects, etc. You want people to *feel* certain emotions.
- **Re-enactment.** This is standard procedure in some police investigations but martial artists do it all the time too. The goal is to recreate an event, in most cases a specific fight or technique you saw used.

To a certain extent, these things get mixed together but they're also mutually exclusive. It's hard to show skill if adding drama to the demonstration is more important. And vice versa, the most dramatic demonstrations have less to do with skill than with good choreography and acting skills. Re-enactment rarely shows the most amount of skill because it also shows everything that went wrong in the fight.

As you can see, these are all very different ways of demonstrating fighting techniques.

Just to illustrate this point a bit more, let's look at two examples:

- When you watch a video of traditional Karate masters, they usually do a crisp and clean demonstration: the demonstration is often very formal and shows primarily technical skills, both physical and mental. Spectacular and dramatic, it is not.
- Look at a video presenting a modern self-defense program or a Reality Based Self Defense system and things will be radically different: there will be either ominous music and sound effects or a heavy metal sound track, the editing emphasizes speed by cutting to another scene every couple seconds, the overall pace of the video is usually high with short action sequences shot from close by and at specific angles, etc. Learning techniques from such a clip is hard because of all this but viewing it will certainly get you in the mood to train with that teacher, which is the whole purpose.

31

Notice how these videos look so much different from what you see in live footage. Demonstrations show you *idealized versions of fights*, or they show only a very limited aspect of them.

Instructional

Now we're finally getting to the ugly little step-child of videos. The one that creates all the problems and misunderstandings.

Instructional videos **teach** you techniques, ideas and concepts. They virtually always include some demonstration sequences as well to give you a better idea of what the material should look like, but that's not the meat of those videos. As with all teaching tools, there are too many styles and approaches to list them all but here are some common points:

- **Slow.** Look at the live footage and pick a technique, any one will do. Then try to teach it *exactly* like that to somebody else. You'll quickly find that even watching it in slow motion doesn't give you all the details you need to teach it correctly. That's why instructional videos show techniques slowly. You learn better that way.
- **Step-by-step:** Every technique consists of several components. A right cross has a step forward, driving off the back leg, a hip turn, torso turn, extension of the arm, slight retraction of the other arm and I'm not even covering the finer points. The purpose of an instructional video is to teach you not only all these steps but show you which sequence they go in and which ones happen simultaneously. Pausing at each step is the best way to point this out.
- **Static camera/best angle.** For better viewing, the camera doesn't move at all and the presenters stay in the frame. The camera is also placed in the best viewing angle to capture the movement. Very often, this means a long shot for most of the instruction and close ups of finer points. This is very helpful for explaining a technique but (especially the long shot) *makes the footage look less impressive* than a dramatic demonstration.

The goal of instructional videos is to give you the information you need to *learn* a technique, the *tools* to practice it and a *demonstration* of what it looks like. No more, no less

On my YouTube channel (search for the channel "ptccm" or just my name and you'll find it), you can view a video clip from my Pad Man DVD. Notice how I do a LOT of talking. Some might say too much and that's OK, but I believe in giving out as much information as I can when I release a book or DVD, so I try to mention everything I think is important for the topic at hand.

Along with explaining how you can hold the Thai pads, I also show everything as clearly as possible:

- I show the position both facing the camera and then sideways.
- When necessary, I switch positions with my partner so my body doesn't hide what I'm pointing out.
- I'll point with the finger of my other hand on the pad to emphasize certain things. Like at 6min11, to point out the slight diagonal angle of the pad.
  The camera comes closer when I'm pointing out these things. It zooms out again when my partner does the technique on the pad. This way, you get both clear instruction and a good view during the demonstration part.

When you watch this video, you'll notice we never hit full power or do long combinations on the pads. Doing so would be a waste of time and videotape because this part of the video is **not** about how to do an intense three min. round on the Thai pads. It's about teaching **how to hold them**. Unfortunately, that means the footage isn't all that spectacular. But if you've never held a pad in your life, information is more important to you than looks. And that's the goal of this video, not how awesome it might look.

Case in point, here's one viewer's comment:
> *my bad , i didn´t read the headline i was focus on the fighters very poor performance.?*
> *But great vid for mitsholders !*

My response:

No worries. My partner in this vid is not a professional fighter or anything like that. He is however a great guy for spending hours on end with me in the studio. Besides, fighters too often want to show off, which is not what you need in an instructional video. You need somebody reliable who takes instruction well so the material gets captured correctly by the camera.

With this comment, we've come full circle with 80KungFu's comment in Part 1: he totally missed the point that in an instructional video, you don't try to recreate *all* the factors of what you see in live footage but *only* the ones needed to give the best possible instruction. That's why the demo partners in these videos often look like dummies just standing there: **they're supposed to do that so you can see what's going on.**

If they would act like real attackers, everybody would be crying over how they can't make out anything on the video they just bought. The instructor would also be forced to crank up the intensity levels of his techniques and there would be a ton of injuries (or worse) on both sides. And you'd still not get any decent instruction. But it would indeed look more "real", I'll admit that...

How to learn techniques from video, Part 3

One of the most common misconceptions of our day is the assumption that the camera tells the truth. We see so many television shows and movies that we become conditioned to believe that what we see is all there is to it. Because "seeing is believing", right?
Nothing could be further from the truth.

What you see in a video is *never* 100% what the instructor/ demonstrator/performer/participant meant to show. Sometimes, he does this on purpose but in most cases, this happens because of the *limitations of video* as an information carrying medium. I'll use my video, the one that started this whole series, as an example.

Camera angle/depth perception.

A good camera man makes or breaks what you put on the screen. If he shoots your best performance from the wrong angle, too close or too far off, you'll still look bad. There are a multitude of camera angles and all of them have a different effect on how you perceive the action:

- Imagine we placed the camera behind my back. How well would you have been able to see the techniques?
- Imagine we only used an overhead camera. It'd be great to see the angle my arms move in but hard to know at what height they're moving.

Depth perception helps you interpret the action you see:

- How far is my fist from the pad when I start each punch?
- What distance does it travel before it lands?

Here's the thing: if the camera angle is poorly chosen, you'll think my punch is either very fast or very slow. It'll look better or worse than what you think a good punch should be. But in reality, my punch went at the speed it did, not the speed you *perceived* when you viewed the clip. Depth perception and a specific camera angles can even be used to make you think a punch lands when in actuality, it doesn't even come close.

Truth be told, you already know this. Every time you see an action movie that doesn't get it right, the fights look "fake". By that I mean the look of things, not the techniques used. So please no comments on how "The Matrix" kung fu wouldn't work in real life. I already know that…

When you show a technique on video, this applies in two different ways:

- The camera angles you need to give good instruction are not always the same as those that make the action look flashy and impressive. Basically, something might look like crap on the screen and still be a great technique in real life.
- If the camera angle is not optimal, you'll miss out on some of the information and not see everything you need to form a good assessment.

Next time you view a martial arts video, remember these technical issues and check if they aren't the cause of your criticism.

Assumptions

In every video, the presenter assumes you know certain things. Simply because he can't explain the full context of the information he's showing. Doing so would mean he'd spend hours and hours talking about it to explain exactly what he means. That just doesn't work in video format. It's great for books and audio, but boring as hell on video.

So the presenter either assumes you know what his goals for the video are or he'll give a brief introduction. But he can never give you all the information you need to make a 100% accurate assessment of his performance. In other words: *you have to do some work to **learn** something from a video.*

The presenter's job is to help you as much as he can but you don't get a free pass. Granted, some people are terrible on screen but even then, you can still learn something if you want to. You just have to start thinking with an analytical mind and follow this rule:

For every point of criticism, find a point of praise.

Look and look again until you find something good whenever you see something you don't like. Here's how you can do this:

- **You're not Ares, God of War.** Start by reminding yourself you don't know everything. You haven't fought every fight, trained in every style nor do you know everything about all things in the universe. In fact, given the hundreds of martial arts and styles out there, you only know very, very little. This applies to me, you and everybody else. In other words, get over yourself.
- **Re-read the previous point.** Put your ego aside, let go of preconceived notions and actually try your absolute best to find positive aspects to this video. Empty your cup, young grasshopper. If your ego protests, tell it you can always say the video is total bullshit *after* you give it an honest viewing. Then you can go back to your regular way of thinking. Doesn't cost you a thing to try this...
- **Imagine the context.** Try to imagine a situation where the technique *could* work: in the ring or the cage, on the street, against a drunk or junkie, against a stronger or slower opponent? Think outside the box and find a place for the technique.
- **Who would benefit?** If you think it's too complicated or too basic, try to figure out who would be able to actually pull off the technique. In other words, who did the instructor have in mind when he showed the technique on video?
- **Look for similarities and differences.** If you see a technique you already know, catalogue the differences between your version and the one in the video. These are often much more interesting than the similarities.

- **Check the parameters.** Look at the footwork, distancing, timing, body mechanics, etc. Analyze the video a separate time for each of these concepts. By viewing through a different filter every single time, you learn more than when you just look at the whole.
- **Fix it.** If all else fails and you can't find anything positive, figure out how you would fix the technique. What would you change to make it work? To make this mental exercise even more useful, try to fix it with the least amount of changes to what is shown in the clip.

With a positive mindset and a wee bit of an effort, you can find loads of interesting ideas and worthwhile information in videos you would otherwise discard out of hand.

Feeling is believing

The one thing video can never bring across is how a technique feels. That's another reason people spit out so many negative comments on YouTube (aside of acting like jerks because they're far away behind the safety of their keyboards, but I digress...) Simply because of the way something looks similar to or different from what they do, they assume it feels a certain way. That assumption can be on the mark, a bit wrong or totally misguided. There's just no way to know for sure until the person in the video does it to you.

Your own experience can actually work against you and serve you some humble pie when you misinterpret how something you see on video will feel in real life. Here are some of the slices I've had to eat over the years:

- Thinking an old school boxer's jab would not pack the same punch as my right cross. Ouch...
- Figuring muay Thai kicks were easy to block after watching a few sloppy fights. (Re-ouch...)
- Looking at silat entries and thinking they couldn't work against heavy punches. (Only half a slice there, but it was a bitter one.)
- Seeing a 140Lbs guy doing push hands and thinking I could easily break his balance. (Hehehehe. Joke's on me.)

If you've been training for a while, you probably ate some of that pie too and know exactly what I mean.

That said, it doesn't have to be a different style than yours for you to fall into this trap. Even within your own style, practitioners have a wide variety of skill levels. Some look like hell on wheels and then turn out to be easy to handle. Other guys, you see them practice and it looks like they're not doing much. But when they hit you, it feels like a ton of bricks just crushed you. And then there's everything between these two extremes, which can mess you up too.

My point is that when you look at a video, remember that **feeling** and *not* seeing is believing.

Missing elements

Remember the Bob Orlando quote about training being simulation? One of the drawbacks of simulations is that **you can never get all the elements of a live situation in it**. There will always be missing elements. For instance:

- You can't simulate a real knife attack when your partner attacks you with a rubber knife. No matter how much you pretend, you know it's not "real". Whatever adrenaline dump you get is likely to be only a fraction of what you'd get in the real thing.
- You can't practice joint breaks 100% on a partner. If you would, you'd be snapping elbows and popping shoulders constantly and nobody would want to play with you anymore. So whenever you're working on those breaks, you're missing out on some really important elements.
- You can't simulate a good punch or kick. If you're training a "punch-block-counter attack" technique, you can't blast your partner's nose through the back of his skull. So how can you know for sure what a real attacker's reaction to your technique would be?

And so on, ad nauseam. This isn't a big deal really. It's just a limitation of training that you have to leave certain elements out of the equation to allow for safe and constructive practice. We all do this when we go to class or practice on a heavy bag: you know you're not doing "the real thing", no matter how close you try to get to it.

This is also a limitation of videos as a medium, similar to the "Assumptions" I mentioned before:

- In an instructional video, you can be relatively thorough in explaining which elements are missing and why.
- In a demonstration video, that's not possible because you're not there to explain anything; you're there to show it and make it look good.

A final aspect to these missing elements is this:

Just because the presenter shows a technique a certain way, that doesn't mean he doesn't know how to do it in other ways. **It only means he chose to show that specific variation and not another one.** If he would show every variation he knows, the video would be too long for its purpose.

So when you see that YouTube video, look for the missing elements and wonder if they were left out on purpose before you comment.

Case in point 1

In this clip, I'll show the same technique from the original one but try to clarify it with the content from this "How To" guide. It's called "Grasping the bird's tail" and comes from tai chi chuan. As always, look for it on my YouTube channel to see what I'm talking about.
Some points:

- You can clearly see which section is instructional and which is demonstration.
- The instructional portion is done step-by-step and I pause at every important point so you can see it well. I also exaggerate the components so the camera can pick them up better.

- The demonstration part adds another element: speed. As you can see, my partner has precious little time to throw a second punch because I go for his lead elbow as soon as I finish checking his rear hand.
- If you look closely, you'll notice I pause slightly when I do that. The reason is my partner's safety. I can do the technique without the pause but then I risk injuring him. Another missing element.
- You'll also see me sometimes hook his elbow with my fingers and other times, go for an elbow break first. That's a personal preference, nothing else.
- Had we placed the camera more to the side, the arm drag would have looked more spectacular. But you would not have had a good view of *how* I did it.

Question: I left out another element to make this technique even more effective. What do you think it is?

Answer: Every single time I do the technique, my right hand checked my partner's left arm but did nothing else. The purpose of doing it that way is to make sure he doesn't get in a punch with that arm as I move into position for my counter. But just *checking* his arm is not the only way to do that technique. A way I vastly prefer is *striking* my opponent with my right hand as I step in. The strike can aim for his arm or shoulder, his chest or (perhaps the best way) his face. The movement looks identical to what you see in the video with one exception: the partner throwing the punch is knocked back or off balance. Which is why I grab his wrist with my left hand as soon as his punch has slowed down enough for me to do so: it keeps him close to me and also extends his arm, making it easier for me to break it or pull him off balance for the hammer fist to the back of his neck.

My students hate it when we train this variation because to them, it feels like running into a wall. This has mainly to do with using the right structure and not as much with how much muscle you use. Trust me on this: it sucks blocky nuts when that palm strike lands just as you fire a full-speed, full-power punch.

Case in point 2

Same deal as before: the technique from the original video with some additions. It's also from tai chi chuan and called "Single whip" on my YouTube channel.
More commentary:

- Once again, I do the instructional vs. demonstration thing. See the previous case for more on that.
- For even better instruction, I should have switched sides with my partner but you already saw that part in the original clip. So I left that element out.
- I add a missing element: impact. By striking the pad, you can see how the impact straightens out the attacker's arm and makes the arm bar easier to do.
- I'm still not even close to how it would work in real life though. I'm not hitting the pad full power because otherwise, it would slam into my partner's face. His ear was already ringing after this short clip, so full power could actually cause injury: another limitation.
- But it does show that if I can land that palm strike, he won't have a good opportunity to launch a second punch.
- In the last arm bar I show, I start putting pressure on him *as* I slide from his shoulder all the way to the elbow. In the previous ones, I had but very light contact with his arm and only applied pressure *when I got to his elbow*. The camera cannot pick this up. The only visual cue you have is how he lands slightly more forward than before. But to my partner, it feels very, very different.

Conclusion

I haven't even scratched the surface with the explanations for these two short clips but that wasn't my goal. The techniques aren't important, the way you view them, how you analyze them and ultimately, the conclusions you come to, that's what counts.
I hope this guide gave you some more insight on how videos work and how you can find useful information if you know what to look for. That was my primary goal in writing it. My other goal was this: explain

once and for all why certain things just don't work well on video and how what you see is not what you get. Now that I'm done, I can link to this article whenever I get another dumb, spiteful or misinformed comment on my YouTube channel.

There are bound to be loads more of those.

Confidence

One of my newer students asked me a question after class, something along the lines of:

You can pretty much handle anybody in the street, right?

I replied with "Not only no, but hell no!" and seemed to get a confused look from him at first. I then explained that in the street, things are pretty different than in class and there are no guarantees. None at all.

Anybody can be taken out at any time. It doesn't matter how good you are, you're not invincible. You can always have an off day and not see it coming. Or sometimes, you just mess up. It happens.

But I understood where his question came form: it's easy for a teacher to look good in class. I'm the one showing everything, explaining how they have to do the techniques and by default I'm the benchmark for my students. I'm **supposed** to be able to pull it off against them. If I can't hack it against them, then I don't really have much business teaching. So I understand why he would think I'd take on a horde of ninjas in a dark alley with one arm tied behind my back.

We talked some more and he explained how the training has made him feel more confident, more secure that if he had to throw a punch, the other guy would at leastfeel it. Which sparked another round of long explanations on my part (my older students groan when they see me get ready for another Castro-length speech...) covering things like adrenal stress, the difference between sports fighting and actual combat, running instead of fighting and so on.

As I drove home that night, I thought about it some more.

It's been a long time since I started training but I remember the feeling you get when things start to come together for the first time:

- A technique you had trouble with suddenly makes sense and you can always pull it offfrom then on.
- The teacher corrects a detail of your technique and suddenly you hit twice as hard.
- You finally nail the guy who always beats you in sparring.

And the list goes on and on. I remember some of those things from my early years. They bring a sudden rush of confidence in your abilities. That's not a bad thing. It keeps you motivated to train hard and stick with the art. But it can also lead you away from the path if the confidence is misplaced or you don't have a sense of proportion:

- What if it only *feels* like you're hitting twice as hard? But in reality your punch hasn't really improved much, you only think it has.
- What if that other guy had a bad day and wasn't concentrated when you nailed him? Next class, he might own you again.

I'm exaggerating a little but you get my point: *Confidence doesn't necessarily have anything to do with your actual abilities.*

Case in point:

I started with judo and ju jitsu when I was 14 years old and never got beyond orange belt. I switched to kung fu after a year and a half of those Japanese arts and never went back. I was about 17 when I went to train at a friend's ju-jitsu school and the teacher there had me spar with two of his black belts. Not knowing any better, I swept them a couple of times and kicked them in the face. I was completely and totally amazed at how easy it was for me to land my shots. I mean, they were Black Belts™!!! And I had only been an orange belt with a few years of kung fu training.

You can bet I felt pretty damn confident after that.

A year later I started competing in full-contact tournaments and got my ass handed to me, repeatedly. It wasn't that I was terrible; there were just *a whole bunch of people who were better.*

This brings us back to my student: those moments when the training goes well and your confidence grows, they're magic. You shouldcherish and enjoy them to the fullest. But right after, you get back to training hard and try to get better. Because there's always somebody better than you. Or, as I explained before, you might be completely overestimating your skills after that confidence-boost hits you.

Either way, there's no other choice but to keep on training. There will always be a ratio of people who are better than you and those who are not. The harder you train, the less there will be of the former and the more of the latter. At least, in theory. In the street, Mr. Murphy can come along any time and mess up your uber-mad skillz in a heartbeat. Which brings up the whole "no guarantee" thing again.

I ended up repeating to my student what one of Loren's instructors told him:

Your training doesn't make you superman. It only gives you an edge.

Truer words were never spoken.

The martial arts student who makes you proud.

One of Kris Wilder's blog posts got me thinking about the many students I've had over the years. You get all kinds of people coming to class and it's your job as a teacher to give it your all so they learn as much as possible. This isn't always easy. Top of my head, this is what I remember of 20 years of teaching martial arts to loads of students:

- Some were good athletes; others were not physically gifted at all. Most people seem to fall in between. I've also been fortunate to have had natural athletes join my class. Those are always a lot of fun to work with because they have energy to spare.
- Most students picked things up OK though a couple had absolutely no co-ordination to speak off. They literally weren't at home in their body, moving as if they were an alien life-form inhabiting it or as if it belonged to somebody else. Very few of those lasted long because no matter what I tried, they always struggled to learn movements the other students picked up easily.
- I had one, just one, super-gifted student. She was a young woman who studied classical piano and was interested in tai chi chuan. When I showed her the first movement of the form, she repeated it perfectly. Then I showed the second and the same thing happened. And so on. It was impressive to see a student just flat out carbon-copy my movements. Unfortunately, she didn't continue because she was afraid of injuring her hands with the self defense techniques and be forced to end her musical career. She could have been amazing.
- Most students were good people but every now and then there was an asshole who wanted to hurt the others. He'd use the sparring sessions to beat up his classmates. When this happened Iput a stop to it but every now and then I had to "teach a lesson". I never enjoyed that but sometimes it was necessary.
- The funniest student was a guy who called me up first to ask about my classes. During that conversation, he told me three times that he was the European MMA cage fighting champ. I congratulated

47

him every time. He also explained his TKD teacher was afraid to spar him now... Oh-kaaaaaay... Anyway, he showed up for my Sanshou class: early thirties, skinny but with a potbelly, balding but with the remaining hair in plucks and a look in his eyes that said "Nobody home, thank you for calling!" We start the warm-up and he's huffing and puffing after 5 min. As soon as we start practicing techniques, I notice he can't lift his leg above waist level and has terrible technique. Maybe he won the EU video game cage fighting competition or something because he sure wasn't a fighter. He then (barely) makes it until the end of the session, walks up to me and pays for ten classes upfront. That was the last time I ever saw him. Weird as he was, it sure was nice of him to sponsor the school like that...

- The student I'm most proud of though wasn't a particularly gifted one. Not good or bad, just average. He did well enough in class, except when we sparred. Then he'd get an enormous adrenal dump and he went nuts:
    o He'd tense up and cross his forearms instead of staying in the on guard position.
    o He'd start to breathe hard through his nose, at the edge of hyper-ventilating.
    o His eyes went wide, he lost almost all his technical skills and flailed all over the place.

It didn't matter how low or high the intensity of the sparring was, he just defaulted to that setting every single time. I tried dozens of things to help him but nothing ever got rid of this problem completely. It ever so slowly got better and in the end, he only lost it when he got tagged hard.

He stayed with me for six or seven years and that's what made me most proud to have him as a student. Because in all those years, he came to class twice a week, **knowing full well he was going to be freaked out and scared out of his mind when we sparred.** *And he showed up anyway.* It takes a special kind of courage and determination to do that.

There were other students like him but I never had anyone who had to conquer his own fears as much. I was sorry to see him go when he eventually quit.

Assholes in the ring

Here's another pet peeve of mine.

There are two schools of thought when it comes to competing:

- Compete to the best of your abilities but do everything you can to stay within the rules.
- Win at all costs, regardless of rules, aka "As long as you can get away with it, it's OK."

I was of the first category when I competed and the opponents I met from the second always pissed me off. First of all, there are rules for a reason:

- It's a game, no matter how hard you punch and kick each other. Games have rules. By entering the competition, you explicitly agree to them. If you don't want to do that in the first place, find another game to play.
- The rules make the game fun. They force you to find solutions for the limitations they create, especially the rules you might not agree with. But they make you a better athlete if you focus on solutions instead of problems.
- They're there to keep you safe. Fighting is dangerous and competitions create a legal and controlled environment to engage in that dangerous behavior. When you break the rules, you start edging towards illegal acts (if you don't flat out break the law already) and control goes out the window. As a result, it's no longer a game. And if you don't want to play a game, then say so before you enter one so we're all on the same page.

The last point is what annoys the hell out of me. If you want to play the fight game, then stick to the rules. If you want to fight without rules: go to the bad part of town, walk up to a street thug and say "I always knew you liked Sponge Bob, you pussy!" You'll have all the fight you want in no time… But that type of competitor usually doesn't want a "fight": he either wants to win at all costs or he wants an excuse to beat somebody up.

Winning, no matter what

When you compete, winning is the best feeling there is. All your hard work pays off and you get a glorious moment in the spotlight. Then there's the afterglow during the next couple days before you start training for the next event. If you're a professional, winning also means lots of money, fame, women, etc.

Put it all together and you have a situation in which competitors want to win *real* bad or feel enormous pressure to do so. Given the right situation, it doesn't take much to turn a fair-play fighter into a mean mo-fo in the ring. So I do understand the dynamic behind it. I disagree, but it's human nature. Especially when there's all that money involved.

However, when there's no financial gain, I don't feel much empathy with the bastard who acts like an asshole in the ring. Case in point:

My very first full-contact competition was an open tournament under kyokushinkai-type rules. I made it to the finals and later found out my opponent's teacher was the referee for our match. That alone qualifies the guy as an asshole. I wouldn't have accepted my teacher doing such a thing (nor would he ever do it but that's beside the point). It was a clear conflict of interest, period.

Anyway, we seemed evenly matched throughout the fight, which was probably why the guy decided to knee me in the balls. It was in plain view of his teacher/referee who didn't call a foul. It pissed me off. I got up and started to pound on the guy as hard as I could. He backed up under the pressure but there wasn't enough time before the end of that last round to finish it. Obviously, the guy won.

That was my first (and certainly not last) encounter with this kind of fighter. I loathe them now just as much as I did then. They just rub me the wrong way. I won't think twice about kicking a field goal into the nuts of an attacker in the street, but I don't feel the need to do so when I compete. If I can make that distinction, so can they.

I also understand about frustration when you fight: giving it your all and you can't put the other guy away. Or he's just using unorthodox techniques that throw you off and all you need is one clean hit, which you just can't seem to find. Been there, done that. But this too is part of the game. You know upfront you'll be in situations like this so if you can't stand it, go play another game instead of acting like an ass.

Beat somebody up

Then there's the other kind, the bully/fighter. They're the guys who like to beat somebody up and find a perfect environment to do so in the ring. There, they can get away with being aggressive without repercussions from the other side (like a baseball bat across the head when you step around the corner.) Some people even praise them for being such impressive "warriors". But in reality, these fighters just look for opportunities to act like a common street thug and not pay a price for it.

Don't get me wrong, they still have to train hard or they'll get owned when the bell sounds. But that doesn't change their mindset of looking for victims instead of opponents. They'll cheat or commit fouls whenever they can get away with it. They'll even ridicule their opponents for being boy-scouts and sticking to the rules.

As you can expect, I loathe these guys just as much as the cheaters. I loathe it even more when they whine like a baby when an opponent turns the tables by using the same fouls or illegal techniques to show they won't put up with that crap. Or when they take it out on the referee or the crowd like a spoiled little brat.

Here are some examples of assholes in the ring:

- *Act like a total douchebag.* Do a search for "Dominique Valera vs. Rick Roufus" on YouTube. This is an old exhibition fight that Rick Roufus did when he was in his prime, age 27. His "opponent", Dominique Valera, was **47** at the time. The whole idea of an exhibition is that it *isn't a real fight*. Both fighters are supposed to shine and entertain the crowd. But if you look close, you'll see Roufus puts a lot of power in his strikes; he doesn't hold back all that much. Valera however never does much more than snap his punches and kicks. In round 1, Rick's jump spin back kick breaks Valera"s ribs but the man continues without complaining. Roufus goes on to repeatedly plow into the Frenchman with heavy middle kicks and punches.

He makes it all about him and humiliates Valera in front of his home crowd. For an exhibition match with a guy who could have been his father, that's some pretty low class behavior.

- *Cheat because you can.* Now do a search for the video "Super Fix Classic." This fight mainly shows the incompetence of the referee: he just lets it all happen unpunished. Hitting after the break, wrestling, guillotine choke, pushing the throat into the ropes, rabbit punches, holding and hitting, the works. The only reason that fighter gets to do all that is because the referee isn't stopping it and he knows it.
- *You just can't help yourself.* Once more: look for "Badr Hari Vs Remy Bonjasky K1 WGP 2008" I don't like Badr Hari. He's a good fighter and all that but he's also a bully, this fight here is just one more example of that fact. He just can't help himself and his street thug mindset shows when Bonjasky slips. Sure, Bonjasky puts on a show but that's beside the point: Hari was frustrated because he got nailed by Remy in the first round and couldn't really pin him down. So he acts like a flaming idiot.

Now I may not be a choir boy but at least I never pulled any crap like that when I competed. Nor do I accept my students to behave like that. Like I said, if you want to use dirty tricks, go pick a fight in a rough neighborhood. But that kind of behavior doesn't have a place in the ring.

Martial arts basics

Another blogger got the ball rolling and asked me to join in. I gave it some thought and here's my take on it.

His premise was that people often neglect the basics of their art because they either don't understand the importance or think they've already done enough of them. Odds are these two reasons form the bulk of what causes the problem. On the other hand, I think that to a certain degree the main fault is always with the teacher. If his students don't have good basics, he's the one who failed to teach them. Though there are exceptions to this.

An example

In my Sanshou class, there is a specific progression when a new student starts:

1. Fighting stance
2. Basic footwork: forward, back, left, right.
3. Straight punches: jab and cross.
4. Straight knees: left and right.
5. Hook punches: left and right.
6. Push kick: back leg and step up with front leg.
7. Round kick: back leg and step up with front leg.
8. One basic throw and takedown.

The student starts by working in front of a mirror, doing ten reps before switching to another technique. As he won't know many techniques in his first couple classes, he'll do hundreds of straight punches before he even gets to the infamous round kick. Which is the whole point; I want to drill the basic techniques in first.

Back in the "good" old days, we'd do hundreds of reps of the same technique, non-stop. That's just the way it was. In Asia, this still seems to be the way it is done in many styles. That's not a bad thing, on the contrary. I'm a firm believer in doing your reps and the quality of movement of a traditionally trained martial artist is often light years beyond what modern practitioners can show. So this method does work.

The other side of the coin is that in Asia, people seem to easily accept the fact that you have to train the same thing over and over. And those who don't aren't allowed to protest and have to do it anyway. In the West, we want to know *why* you do things a certain way and we want to have our say in the matter. If you try to teach the Asian way over here, you usually end up with very, very few students.

Some people say that for the sake of tradition, you should never adapt your teachings to your audience. I think that's nonsense. I believe you get better results by a combination of ingraining basics with lots of reps but also by adding slight variations as soon as a student performs them well enough.

Back to the example.

It takes about three months before a new student in my sanshou class is ready to join the group. However, that doesn't mean they can only practice the seven points I listed before. As soon as they have a basic mastery of those, they also practice:

- Combining the techniques with footwork: stationary striking vs. stepping forward as they strike.
- Basic 1-2 combinations with those techniques: jab-cross, jab-knee, etc.
- One basic defense against each of these techniques.
- Basic defense plus counter for each technique.
- Working with a partner who moves around slowly.
- Working on the heavy bag and other equipment.

It varies from one student to another but most of them can absorb these additions pretty easily. The goal is to have the students practice each of the 8 points from my basics list, non-stop for two to three months. Every class starts with revising everything they learned so far (getting the reps in) and then I add one (or several) of the additions from the second list, always checking to see if they can keep up.

This way, they automatically get their reps in but do so in a way that offers tons of variation. *At the same time*, it prepares them for what they'll need to learn *after* they master the basics. Because as they're learning these techniques, I start giving them the basic strategies and tactics inherent to the sport and then explain guidelines to learn them:

- **Basic strategy:** hit the other guy and don't get hit.
- **Basic tactic:** either you're attacking, or you're moving out of range. Don't be in range and just stand there doing nothing.
- **Basic training guideline:** As soon as you can do so in a technically correct manner, step forward *as* you attack and step away *as* you retract the last technique.

Every tactic and strategy they'll learn after that is built upon their ability to understand and perform these three basic points. It's only very late in their development as a fighter that I teach them when, why and how to break these rules.

From the get go, the whole process of learning is streamlined to bring them to a point of mastering the basics (at a beginner level) as soon as possible. That means they have to train a certain way, do things in a certain order, every single class. As this structure makes them work the basics over and over (though every time in a slightly different way), progress is usually fast. To avoid messing up this whole process, they are not allowed to improvise unless I explicitly tell them to.

Again, it all fits in a larger whole and as long as they aren't technically proficient enough, as much fun as it can be, free-wheeling only slows down their progress. Basics come first.

It isn't always honey and rainbows.

That said, not every student gets it and sometimes, I can't change that. Some of them see the class as just one of the things they do in their lives. They're just filling their time and using up oxygen. Most of those don't last long in my class because they don't want to put the effort in. That's OK by me; I changed my approach to teaching a while ago to this:

- Everybody trains for different reasons. Some of these are similar to or the same as mine, others have different ones. As a teacher, I'll try and help all students, regardless of their motivations to come to class.
- However, I expect students to do as instructed to the best of their abilities, whatever these may be. If they don't, then I'll try to explain them the reasons why this is important. Or at the very least say "It'll avoid problems later on in your practice of the art."
- Students who take instruction well and practice hard get more material and information to work with. Those who don't get very little new information, if any. Each student decides for himself how hard he works so the pace of his progress is determined by him and not me.

If at the end of the day, a student doesn't have solid basics then he's either going to have to keep working on them in class, not learning much else. Or he'll eventually drop out. Not only because he'll get tired of practicing those basics (regardless of how much variety I put in there), he'll also be unable to perform any technique that is slightly more difficult than a "mere" basic. All the other students, the ones who did train as instructed, will have no problem with such techniques.

Martial arts basics, Part 2

In the first part of "Martial arts basics", I talked about how I like to teach my students the importance of basic techniques by making them do loads of repetitions. The key is, once they have a good enough grasp of the techniques, to make those reps challenging and fun by adding slight variations and tweaks. In this video, I'll show you how I personally like to train and what my students have to do too.

Before you read on, watch the video called "How to train basic punches on the heavy bag" on my YouTube channel.

A couple of things:

- I'm not focusing on speed or power but on technique. My focus is on working those basics and studying the differences between each variation.
- I picked the four basic punches because that's what we were working on in class. It could have been other techniques, so don't get hung up on that part.
- The bag was hanging a bit too low and as a result, it moved around too much. Instead of stopping it with a technique (which requires a different type of timing from what I was working on), you'll see me slow down or even grab the bag. This is something I don't do often. Usually, I time a punch or kick to stop it in its tracks. Ideally, you have a partner holding the bag for you.
- Obviously, you need to do the same drill with a partner to transfer what you practiced on the heavy bag to actually using those skills on an opponent.
- This is by no means the only way to train your basics. I'm just showing a possible example of how you *can* go about it so it's fun as well as productive. I could have done it in a hundred different ways or chosen tons of other variations.
- The important thing isn't how I do the techniques or which particular variations I chose. What matters is that there **is** a

progression instead of just hitting the bag with whatever you think off at the moment. There's a place for free-style training but also for more structured training like in this clip.

It doesn't matter if you practice combat sports or a traditional art; you can use the same format to have more fun drilling in your basics.

MMA sucks, traditional martial arts suck more.

The title covers a typical exchange between the MMA and traditional martial arts crowds when they start arguing. Usually, the arguments are something like this:

- You need to know how to fight at all ranges, including the ground.
- MMA is "real" because there are minimal rules and traditional arts suck because they don't fight for "real".
- Traditional arts are better because they focus on fighting without rules and the techniques are ultra-mega-instantly lethal.
- MMA doesn't protect you against multiple opponents or weapons. In fact, MMA tactics get you killed in those situations.

And so on ad nauseam. Now at face value, all of these points are valid. There's something to be said for each of them and to a degree, you can't really fault the logic behind them. There's just one thing: they're all totally missing the point. As in, missed it by a mile. More on that later.

This kind of bickering reminds me of the old arguments of judo vs. wrestling or boxing about 50-60 years ago. Later on karate hit the scene and it was compared to those too. This happened with every "new" martial art or combat sport to hit the big time over the decades. Just page through a few martial arts magazines of 20-30 years ago and read the articles. You'll find it's all there.

With the rise of the Internet, things got worse. I'm old enough to have been training in the arts before there were chat rooms and bulletin boards. If you are too, you know what I mean. If you're not, here's some perspective: It used to be a big-ass argument who would beat the other in a real fight: Bruce Lee or Chuck Norris. We all know what happened on film at the Coliseum but what if they'd have gone at it for real?

There were long arguments about how Chuck had won dozens of tournaments where Bruce never competed in anything so he sucked. The kung fu lovers would counter that Chuck only fought within rules where as Bruce had plenty of street fighting experience where anything goes. These are only two of the arguments; there were many, many more.

But doesn't this ring a bell for you? Compare this to the latest fad in martial arts land, MMA, and look at the type of arguments I listed in the first paragraph. It's the same type of logic, over and over again. The inherent flaw is the lack of an overall picture regarding violence. My position on it is that there are a few crucial elements missing in the logic chains. Here's what I said elsewhere:

I train mostly in Chinese MAs. I have yet to find one that has anything resembling BJJ or any other ground fighting system. All that I've seen is moves to get the other guy off/away from you and get up. Shuai Jiao (Chinese wrestling) has almost no techniques where you go to the ground to throw somebody (I know of only one but there might be more). Everything else is just putting the guy down and not following him.

Sanda/Sanshou matches allow all sorts of striking and throwing but no ground work. You get a penalty if you aren't on your feet in three seconds after a throw, even if you're the one throwing your opponent. You also fight on a platform, forcing you to take your environment into account. If you get tossed of the stage twice, you lose the round. And even though there are often soft mattresses around the stage, it can still hurt big time to fall off. I've seen broken arms and guys flying into their coaches sitting a long way off as they were kicked off the stage.

All that to say this:

Maybe, just maybe there's a reason why fighting arts in China don't go to the ground… The way I learned it, if you fall on the ground, you die. No quarter was given nor expected. You got stomped to death, stabbed, speared, chopped up or run over by horses.

So your goal was to not fall and if you did, to get up as fast as you can. If you wanted to control somebody without hurting, you did the chin na (joint locks) every frikkin' Chinese style forces you to learn.

The whole key to the previous paragraphs is context. Context is king when fighting is involved. I'll explain in a bit, here's some more.

Rules make the fight. Here's the list of fouls in the UFC:

- Butting with the head.
- Eye gouging of any kind.
- Biting.
- Hair pulling.
- Fish hooking.
- Groin attacks of any kind.
- Putting a finger into any orifice or into any cut or laceration on an opponent.
- Small joint manipulation.
- Striking to the spine or the back of the head. (see Rabbit punch)
- Striking downward using the point of the elbow.
- Throat strikes of any kind, including, without limitation, grabbing the trachea.
- Clawing, pinching or twisting the flesh.
- Grabbing the clavicle.
- Kicking the head of a grounded opponent.
- Kneeing the head of a grounded opponent.
- Stomping a grounded opponent.
- Kicking to the kidney with the heel.
- Spiking an opponent to the canvas on his head or neck. (see piledriver)
- Throwing an opponent out of the ring or fenced area.
- Holding the shorts or gloves of an opponent.
- Spitting at an opponent.

Funny thing how these are the exact same things many traditional Chinese arts will turn to **first** against a grappler. They won't go for a sprawl and turn to a mount position simply because *they don't want to be on the ground*. They'll try to wrench the guy's neck while they rip his lips off and gouge out an eye. Easy to say then that traditional arts are crap in the Octagon. *They weren't made for that environment.* Duh…

This is just one aspect of context. Now let's follow this line of thinking a bit further:

The UFC is not the only MMA game around. Take a look at Pride and you'll see differences in the way they fight. The critical difference in rules is this:

- Pride allows kicking and kneeing the head of a downed opponent who is on his back. This is considered a foul in the Unified Rules, which only allows kicks and knees to the head of a standing opponent. Nowadays, you even see UFC fighters touch the floor with their fingers when they're in a clinch against the fence so their opponents aren't allowed to kick or knee them in the face.
- Pride allows a fighter to stomp the head of a downed opponent. This is considered a foul in the Unified Rules.
- Pride allows a fighter to Spike (pile driver) an opponent. This is considered a foul in the Unified Rules.

As soon as the stomping and soccer kicks start on a downed opponent, you see a totally different fight. The stompee goes into defensive mode by turtling up or bringing his legs in front, he tries to close the distance to grab the stomper's legs and most of all; **he looks for an opening to get up**. I've yet to see one of these situations turn into anything but a frantic attempt at not getting knocked out… I'd like to offer this as exhibit A in my thesis that traditional arts have it right about not wanting to go to the ground…

And there it is: *change just a couple of rules and the tactics and techniques that work best change too*. When you allow striking a downed opponent, this has a huge impact on the fight game. It forces you to react differently as soon as you hit the ground. Pretty much like in a real street fight…

Now before you MMA fans starts howling for my blood, here's some more:

I love MMA and trained in shoot fighting for a while; I had a blast there and would have continued to this day if the teacher hadn't moved. But martial arts and combat sport styles (like MMA) are just tools. They work great within a certain context and not so in others. Of course there is overlap but as Randy said, *the differences are just as important.*

People should get over themselves and learn to live and let live.

I don't see any military men arguing that the techniques and tactics for arctic warfare are better/worse/easier/etc. than those employed in the desert or in an urban environment. They seem to instinctively grasp the idea that snowshoes are great to speed up a foot soldier on snowy terrain but not so hot for cruising the streets of Fallujah... I've yet to see an argument break out over this. But a lot of martial artists seem unable to follow that line of thinking and apply it to their respective fighting arts.

I believe that context (environment) overrules everything you might think about how a fight should go. One small difference in context can force a totally different set of techniques on you. I really, for the life of me, can't understand why it's so hard to accept that. But apparently the egos and political crap are more important for a lot of folks. To each his own I guess.

And that's where it all comes together. Traditional arts come from a totally different time and context. China 500 years ago was not like Boise, Idaho in 2011. You can't just transpose the arts from that era to today. It doesn't work like that, life is different today. Back then you either learned to take care of yourself or you died:

- There was no local PD like we have now. You couldn't just call for a bunch of cops to come over and deal with the gang of looters/thieves/pillagers/bandits that came to town. Either you hid/ran and didn't get caught or you fought.
- If you fought and lost, you probably died.
- If you fell down you probably got trampled by horses, speared, stabbed with a sword or stomped. And probably died.
- If the fight with one guy took too long, his buddies would help him out and you probably died.
- If you survived and were injured, chances were you ended up

crippled or still died. Medicine then was **not** what it is now. Look up the mortality rate today and then for every decade before the 1900's. You'll see what I mean

- In event of a natural disaster, you took charge or you died. There was no fire brigade, National Guard or rescue team coming.
- There was no social security or health care like today. You got sick, injured, ran out of food; you probably died.

When you consider all these factors (and the list is much longer but I won't go into it now), think of how stupid it would be for a Chinese guy from that era to spend his time learning a submission fighting system. It wouldn't make any sense at all. If you showed him those moves, he'd shake his head and figure you're just a crazy gwailo…Simply because in that time and context, *fighting on the ground was **not** what you did to survive*. Survival was a daily concern for most folks in those times. They didn't need adrenal based scenario training because every day life gave them plenty of that already.

The problem with the whole discussion of MMA vs. traditional arts is this: in many, many contexts outside of the cage or octagon, you still don't want to go to the ground:

- Any type of war or armed conflict involving hundreds/thousands of participants. A soldier never fights alone so going to the ground with one of them gets you killed by his buddies.
- Any fight where weapons are involved. Or *could* be involved because you never know upfront what the other guy brings to the dance. A slit throat while you're going for an arm bar is not a good thing.
- Any environment that puts you at risk when you go to the ground: rocky terrain, concrete, debris filled terrain, etc. You can hit your head when you slam into the floor, he can slam it into the concrete for you, grab a rock/bottle/whatever to mess you up, etc.

These are just a couple of criteria, the list is longer than that but I'm just trying to make a point here: it's not MMA vs. TMAs. That's like arguing if a hammer is better than a screwdriver. They're both tools and have their limits/uses. You don't hear carpenters arguing over which is better, right?

In my opinion and experience, it's the same with fighting arts. They're tools and as such useful in some areas while not so much in others. Pick one you like and know where it works well while not ignoring the weaknesses. Feel free to disagree though, I'm OK with my own choices and you should be with yours. It's your ass on the line when that crazy maniac swings a tire iron at your head, not mine.

Just as a parting shot: A soldier on active duty in a not so nice part of the world, a guy who converts people from living to dead said this:

Anybody know of a weapon (other than the rifle) that is best used from the ground?

That one sentence sums up the whole point I tried to make here. I can think of no personal weapon that is specifically designed to work better from the ground than standing up. Let's expand on that and look at all weapons throughout the history of mankind. I can't find any examples. So maybe, just maybe, there is a good reason why going to the ground in a violent conflict is not always a good thing…

MMA sucks, traditional martial arts suck more, Part 2

I hadn't really intended to write a second part to this post but the amount of reactions I received pushed me to it; so it's all your fault!

Seriously, I seem to have given the impression that I dislike MMA. Despite having clearly stated otherwise, this is still the response I got the most. So I'll repeat it: **I have nothing against MMA, at all.** On the contrary, if I had more time, I'd resume my shootfighting training because I enjoyed it immensely. What's more, I have tremendous respect for everybody who steps into the ring, cage or onto a lei tai. Those who haven't fought full contact (I don't care which rules, it all hurts)don't know what they're talking about and should at the very least respect the courage these athletes show. Which brings us to my first point:

Pressure testing

Over at another blog, somebody commented and said this:

I agree with what you say "What works, works." the rub is how you KNOW it works or not. The traditional arts you espouse lack aliveness, they lack pressure testing, and their students do not KNOW if they can perform the techniques, nor do they KNOW the technique will work of they do.

The training methods are faulty. Embrace it, change the way you train, be a better Martial Artist for it.

This is a classic argument against TMAs and one that I can only half agree with. First what I disagree with:

The argument is based on a false premise: *Some* TMA schools lack anything resembling pressure testing. Many *other* schools have a variety of ways to do so. So it's a statistical issue more than anything else: it depends on which traditional schools you see. Some of the schools I trained at had an insane amount of pressure testing with all-out sparring and no limits to the techniques you could use. There was no protective gear either; they thought gloves and shin guards were for wussies.

In contrast, I've also seen watered-down MMA programs implemented in commercial dojos to increase the income stream. There was no pressure testing at all and the techniques were taught in the same robotic fashion as their traditional arts. Had these people entered a class of that traditional school, they would have been humiliated by the traditional folks, using nothing but their old-school techniques.

So let's say it's way too easy to look at a handful of traditional schools and MMA gyms and then make a blanket statement like that.

Context is king

Here's the part where I agree with that statement.

I mentioned this in the "MMA sucks" post and it's one of the traps traditional folks fall into: You cannot take a traditional art out of its historical/cultural context and expect it to work in another one. Like I said, life in China 500 years ago is not the same as today in the suburbs. You can't just switch these around and expect them to work flawlessly.

But there's a flip side to this: Your art was perhaps developed back then and made you devastatingly lethal for that era. But that doesn't mean you can get those same skills by just going through the motions today. The training methods and concepts will be closed to you until you take your training to a deeper level. What you need most of all is a deep understanding of what violence is. This isn't out of your reach by default as it largely depends on your environment and past experience. There are a only a couple of ways you can get this understanding, which is the common denominator of all the martial components of traditional martial arts:

- Live in a society where violence is a daily occurrence, a fact of life.
- Failing that, having experienced the physical and psychological effects of violence in your past. The more experience, the more understanding you'll have.
- If that isn't the case for you either, you'll need to study, train hard and go through as much pressure testing and scenario training as you can.

Fortunately, most of us live in a society where violence is if not rare, at least not something you face on a day-to-day basis. Sure, you might read or hear about it, but it doesn't **happen to *you*** every single day. As a result, most of us fall into that last category, the ones who have to train hard to get that understanding of what real-world violence is actually like.

The traditional practitioners I mentioned before are all guys who know violence intimately because of where they live or because of their profession. They don't need pressure testing because they get that enough in their daily lives. They understand the realities of violence on a gut level and play for keeps.

If there is anything missing in the way traditional martial artists view their practice, it's often just that: a lack of comprehension of what real violence entails in the practitioner's daily environment. If they would know just a fraction of what happens out there, they would train a whole lot harder. In contrast, most MMA gyms understand the need for rough training to prepare a fighter for the Octagon. And that's where the discord often starts.

From the Octagon to the Street

This is an article I wrote for the January 2009 issue of Black Belt Magazine. I edited it a bit and cut it down for size so it would work better for this book.

"From Mixed Martial Arts to the Street: Practical Grappling Skills for Real-Life Self- Defense" by Wim Demeere

The first Ultimate Fighting Championship in 1993 started a revolution in martial arts competitions: Very few techniques were prohibited and pretty much anything was allowed:

- Vicious elbows to the face.
- Joint locks carried out to the fullest.
- Strikes to the back of the head
- Even kicking a downed opponent.

But the biggest upset was the fact that having a ground game and solid grappling skills proved an absolute necessity to leave the Octagon a winner. The Gracie family demonstrated the effectiveness of its ju-jitsu ground techniques by placing one of their lightest fighters (Royce Gracie weighed a whopping 175 lbs.) against primarily heavyweight opponents. More often than not he managed to submit or choke out his opponents with almost disheartening ease.

Nowadays, MMA competitors no longer fear the ground and have become well-rounded, professional athletes. They are masters of full-power striking techniques, grappling, groundwork, and most of all; they flow effortlessly from the one to the other when the situation demands it.

69

This makes them formidable opponents and places MMA as one of the most versatile combat sports in the world.

The sport itself also changed; it turned into a multi-million dollar industry, eclipsing boxing and other martial arts in popularity. With the increased public awareness came a rise in misconceptions about not only the sport but martial arts and violence in general. The cage is viewed by many practitioners as *the ultimate proving grounds for martial art styles*. They argue that if exponents of any given system cannot beat an opponent in the cage or Octagon, then that system is worthless. They reason that MMA fighters have proven they can take down anyone who solely uses traditional martial arts techniques and then beat or submit them with ground fighting. The seemingly obvious conclusion is that the Mixed Martial Artist is the ultimate fighter in both the cage and the street.

But is this statement true?

To a certain extent, it most certainly is:

- Mixed Martial artists are comfortable fighting at punching and kicking range as well as clinching and stand-up grappling. This places them on equal footing with striking arts like karate, taekwondo or grappling arts like judo and wrestling.
- But their specialty is taking the fight to the floor and working from there until an opponent is knocked out or submitted.

This makes MMAs one of the most effective systems for unarmed dueling. But unarmed dueling categorizes only a fraction of all violent encounters in today's world. There is a much wider variety of situations in which fighting skills are needed:

- Multiple-opponent attacks
- Rape
- Armed aggression
- Violent assault
- Robbery
- Etc.

In most of these environments, taking the fight to the floor is not the best solution. The strategies and techniques that work so well in the Octagon can get you injured or killed in the street. This *doesn't* mean they are useless for self-defense, on the contrary. It does mean *you need to adapt your training to the viciousness of the pavement arena.*

Multiple opponents

When you fight in the cage, you concentrate on the opponent in front of you; there are no other dangers or distractions. However, street crime routinely involves multiple attackers. They usually hide their numbers by making you focus on one aggressor while the others ambush you from behind. If you get clobbered over the back of the head with a tire iron, it doesn't matter how well you can fight in a competition; you will go down. Or the attacker might only reveal his presence after you successfully took the first aggressor to the ground. While you're feeling ecstatic about gaining the mount position on him and are about to do some "ground & pound", you don't see the second man ready to tear into you.

You can avoid all this by:

- Being aware of your surroundings and making it a habit to register the people around you wherever you go.
- If you spot a tough guy scoping you out, immediately assume he's not alone and look for his accomplice(s).
- This tactic applies in spades whenever a stranger approaches you: before he can reach you, sneak a quick peek behind you to spot anyone closing in.
- If you can't prevent the encounter and have to defend yourself, step away from your aggressor as soon as he's down and do a 360° scan to make sure you are safe.

Gender

Once a fight is taken to the ground in the Octagon, it quickly turns into a contest of physical abilities. Unless a competitor places a joint lock or submission just right and with blinding speed, he has to struggle to reach a dominant position from which he can finish it off. This takes a considerable amount of raw strength; a physical attribute the average man has the advantage of over a woman. This places women at a distinct tactical disadvantage on the floor. For instance, violent rape often occurs with the perpetrator pinning his female victim on the ground with his bodyweight and superior strength. Unless the woman has superior grappling skills, her attacker's strength prevents her from getting back on her feet.

Effective women's self-defense courses cover the ground game but they take a different approach from mixed martial arts: instead of trying to beat or submit the attacker, they create opportunities to escape from the ground and get back up again as soon as possible. They use techniques that are not allowed in most MMA tournaments: attacking the eyes, throat, and groin, breaking fingers, biting, or even clawing and ripping skin off. These techniques are meant to disorient and injure the attacker long enough for the woman to get him off of her and escape to safety. Under no circumstances should women try to prolong the fight on the ground by going for a submission or chokehold.

Getting up and away is the best strategy.

Time

In MMA tournaments a joint lock or choke hold rarely works instantly. Competitors transition from one technique to the other for several minutes (or much longer) to finish the fight and often the fighter who appears to be in a difficult position manages to reverse the situation in his favor. In a street confrontation, a fight often takes less than just one minute; *sometimes it's even less than three seconds.*

Usually one side gains the advantage over the other in the first few seconds and then exploits it to incapacitate his opponent. This makes time a critical component for ground fighting in the street; the faster you end the fight, the less chance of something going wrong:

- There are no breaks to catch your breath between rounds or a referee to let you recover from an illegal blow.

- You might just get tired before your attacker does and be unable to finish him off.

This means the *safest* strategy in the street is to incapacitate the attacker in matter of seconds once you hit the floor:

- Instead of struggling for a dominant position that only prolongs the fight, try to get back on your feet before your aggressor does. This always gives you the option to run away if you find yourself facing a stronger opponent or if he brought his friends along to send you to the hospital.
- If you do find an opening for a grappling technique, you might actually have to break or dislocate a joint before you effectively stop your attacker. Don't expect him to tap out or if he does, respect the tap. He might decide to come at you again but this time with much more determination and viciousness.
- Most of all you need to focus your training towards *quick execution and decision making*. That means going for the joint lock with the intent to end the fight in an instant but also the alertness to abandon that same technique if it doesn't work right off the bat. At that point in time, instead of continuing to grapple on the floor, try to get away from your opponent *before* he can hurt you.

Weapons

The days of Roman gladiators butchering each other with swords and other weapons for the entertainment of the people are fortunately in the past. In today's arena, MMA fighters take on each other with empty hands. But things are different on the street: criminals, thugs or violent drunks can and will use weapons to end a fight in their favor. This especially applies to ground fighting. As mentioned above, it usually takes time to choke somebody out or break the joint of a resisting opponent. If your attacker gets to his knife or firearm before you can render him harmless, your chances of survival drop considerably.

U.S. Marines currently train in ground fighting too, but with a specific

73

mindset: they assume their enemy is always armed, regardless of the situation or environment. To instill this mindset, drill instructors place a stun gun in the pockets of some soldiers when they practice ground grappling. This forces recruits to control their opponent and try to finish the fight quickly. If they don't, the stun gun (symbolizing a knife or firearm) gives them a shocking reminder of how real-life fighting can turn deadly in a matter of seconds.

You can train in the same way by:

- Practicing ground fighting in street clothes and incorporating training knives and guns in the sparring sessions. Alternate bouts with both you and your partner armed and then just one of you, practicing both the offensive and defensive aspects.
- Find ways to quickly draw your training weapon before your partner can finish a choke hold or joint lock on you, but also work on preventing him from doing the same.
- In either case, your goal is to get up and away from your armed opponent without delay.
- The other side of this coin is preventing him from disarming you. Conventional stand-up weapon retention techniques don't work as well on the ground, forcing you to adapt them for the ground.

Legal limitations

Self-defense regulations vary from one country to the other and even from state to state. Though there is no single set of laws that is universally applicable across the globe, most justice systems have two essential components: duty to escape and proportionate defense:

- In layman's terms, you have to avoid a physical altercation if that is at all possible. If not, then you are only allowed enough use of force to allow your escape and no more.
- The second concept obligates you to take into account the level of aggression: if an unarmed attacker slaps you in the shoulder, you are not allowed to shoot him until you run out of ammo. The defensive actions you use must be proportionate to his attack.

Though different legal systems interpret and apply these ideas in a variety of ways, they are consistently present.

As a mixed martial artist you can find yourself in legal trouble real fast even though you might be justified in defending yourself. It's hard to argue self defense when witnesses swear they saw you take your attacker down and then rain a flurry of elbow strikes to his face, continuing long after he fell unconscious. Or you might do a perfect throw on an aggressive drunk, pound away at his face for a while and then perform an arm bar that snaps his elbow clean. When he sues you for all you're worth, his lawyer will have a field day painting you as a violent thug who crippled a helpless victim. Odds are good he'll win the case and ruin you financially or send you to prison.

These are just two examples of how things can go wrong but there are many more. MMA competition training is first and foremost a dueling environment. Self-defense is an entirely different animal and the legal system doesn't forgive you for not distinguishing between the two. So when you train ground techniques for self-protection, do so with the goal of ending the fight fast so you can get up and escape.

Conclusion

MMA is perhaps the most spectacular and entertaining combat sport of our time. It is also a great way to get in top physical shape while improving both your health and self-esteem. But whenever you want to use it for self-defense there are certain parameters to take into account. Overall, this is more a matter of *having the right mindset* than a technical issue. Train to understand *the differences between the cage and the street* and then adapt your skills accordingly. Hopefully, you can then continue to live a safe and rewarding life in the knowledge that your fighting skills will be there for you when needed.

From the Octagon to the Street, Part 2

After re-reading my "MMA sucks" post and the first part of "From the Octagon to the Street", there doesn't seem much left for me to say on this topic. I tried to argue my points clearly, citing my reasoning and how I came to those specific conclusions. At this point, like Austin Powers says "I'm spent".

The sad thing about the Internet is how so many people only read two sentences and then pass judgment on an entire article. They form their conclusions based on limited information and then can't wait to vent their disapproval or even anger in the comments section. This is the same thing as watching the first two minutes of a movie and then feeling qualified to praise or bash it... Maybe this is caused by increasingly limited attention spans or information overload, I'm not sure really. Regardless, it seems to become increasingly prevalent as time goes by.

In the real world, there are often no easy explanations. Virtually every topic you could care to discuss is complex and so are the answers to the questions regarding them. That means you have to put a lot of components on the table to give an accurate reply, showing both the forest and the trees. The next part is then exploring how they interact with each other and only then can you start formulating conclusions.

I like that approach. When a given subject matter captures my interest, I want to know everything about it and especially the "Why?" instead of only the "How?" That's just how my mind works and it probably shows in the way I write. In contrast, I absolutely loathe the "Elevator pitch" mentality. Sure, it has some benefits but it needs to be followed up by research and study to see if your original assessment is even in the ballpark. All too often, that's just not the case.

I guess I'm getting older because I don't have much drive anymore to explain the concept of rational debate to those who are only interested in screaming *"It is so because I tell you so!"* Or worse: *"It is so because my great-mega-ultra-grandmaster says so!!!"* I have even less patience with those who spout off an opinion while being too lazy to even think it through or research it:

- Thinking it through means you know exactly why you come to a conclusion: If you used a MMA takedown followed by some ground and pound in every street fight you were in, then it makes *perfect* sense for you to think MMA is the best thing ever for self defense. It is true for *you* because *your* experience proves it. *Nobody* can deny that.

- But if you're then too lazy to research street violence and discover that in a lot of situations, your MMA techniques will sometimes not work, make things worse or get you killed, then you're missing the point. If you *consciously refuse to look deeper,* well, then you're just plain stupid…

- Please bear in mind that *I didn't said MMA techniques **don't** work in the street.* If you understood that from my words, re-read the previous paragraph again; I specifically point out they did just that for you.

- The problem is that it's *just* you, and not everybody else. Even if you go looking at what your friends from the MMA gym do in the street, that still doesn't mean you're right in assuming it's the best thing since sliced bread. As a friend of mine, The Mad Chemist, likes to say *"The plural of anecdote is not evidence."* Mind you, it also doesn't mean you're wrong in your assumptions. My point is, *it doesn't prove anything either way.*

- At the same time, it also doesn't mean that I'm right/wrong. It only means I do the best I can to make sense of it all and reserve the right to change my mind. Which brings the debate full circle.

In the end, you can only work with your personal experience, reasoning and research to come to your conclusions. For each of us, this will be different. I know what I did when I had to fight and I'm pretty certain it will differ from what other people did. It'll also be very similar to what even more others did. The deciding vote then goes to the research and training you do. Which once again will be different for everybody.

This process eventually leads you to a certain set of choices regarding your training. There's only so much time you can train each day and you can't learn every single martial art out there. So what exactly you do train in and how you do so is your own, personal choice. My goal here is to point out that it needs to be a *conscious* decision, one you evaluate regularly, instead of just leaving it to chance and training in whatever random way you happen to end up with. If you make it a conscious choice, you'll be happy with not only your training and your progress but it's also likely you'll be more effective in the street because of it.

Speaking only for myself, I'm happy with my choices even though I'm never quite satisfied with the results. I always try to get better and keep on training, knowing full well there's no such thing as perfection or guarantees. But that doesn't mean you shouldn't try to keep on improving on what you know and learn what you don't know.

MMA against multiple opponents

Jake Shields, Jason "Mayhem" Miller, Nick Diaz and bunch of others get into a brawl at the Strikeforce: Nashville event in April 2010. With some YouTube skills, you'll quickly find the footage. It's not really the image MMA wants to portray to the world but brawls like this happen at martial arts tournaments and fight nights all over the world. What else can you expect when people who like to fight and those who like to watch fights get together? Sooner or later, the excrement hits the rotating blades…

This brawl does however illustrate one thing exceedingly well: I've commented on mixed martial arts for self defense in the past and one of the key points is that MMA has some serious drawbacks when you go up against multiple opponents. This brawl proves exactly that. Now obviously MMA purists might argue that Miller:

- Wasn't really trying to hurt anyone, it was all a promotional stunt.
- Didn't know it would turn into a multiple opponent situation so he wasn't prepared.
- There are no reliable techniques against multiple opponents.
- Some other excuse.

I'd answer with:

- Who knows? I don't think it was a stunt though. I also doubt he enjoyed being manhandled, punched and kicked by four, five people at the same time.
- Well, that's how real violence (as opposed to combat sports) works: you don't get time to prepare.
- Maybe, maybe not. But training to go to the ground in such a situation is usually the worst thing you can do.
- Whatever. The footage speaks volumes.

Here's what I saw in that brawl:

- Miller gets pushed back and the brawl is on.
- Immediately, four, five people start punching, pulling, and pushing him to the floor. He's clearly overwhelmed by these attacks.
- After a few seconds, he's on the floor trying to turtle up.
- He gets kicked while he's there and also receives a couple short shots to the back/kidneys.
- He's only able to get up *after* some of his attackers are pulled off. Until that time, he was ***helpless***.

Now as much as I like MMA as a sport, you clearly see the drawbacks against multiple attackers.

Here's the thing: You can argue any point you like but Miller is not an amateur or crappy MMA fighter. He has a good fight record and is a pretty decent fighter. Also, he's a professional; MMA is his job.
Now for the real question:

If a good, professional MMA fighter can't make it work against multiple attackers, who can?

To me, it's blatantly obvious that training in MMA as a sport has some huge benefits when you want to learn self defense. But as I've stated so many times before, there are some huge differences between the Octagon and the street. Differences you only find out about when you make that transition. But by the time you realize there's something missing in your training (for instance when some thug stabs a blade at your gut) it will be too late to do anything about it. Facing multiple opponents falls into this very category

Once you have more than one opponent, the game changes radically and this presents a problem: if you've only trained for dueling in the cage, fighting one-on-one, then that's what you're specialized in. Your training has ingrained your techniques, strategies and tactics to such a degree you don't have to think about them. In other words, it all goes automatically. This is as it should be because when you fight, you don't have time to debate if you should throw a jab or a leg kick. By the time you make up your mind, your opponent will have you in a rear naked choke. So ingraining techniques into the sub-conscious level is the right thing to do.

But there's a problem with that.

Like I said, what works against one opponent doesn't always work against multiple opponents. Some specific things do, but not everything. Until you specifically train to and/or go out and fight a bunch of guys all together, *you won't know which ones transfer from the Octagon to the street.* Just like you need to ingrain techniques for them to work in the cage, *you need to do the same thing* for fighting multiple attackers in the street.

That's what this brawl illustrates so well: Miller **has** done the ingraining process for fighting in the cage. But as soon as he was out of this environment and faced more than one opponent, he was lost and got beat up. Unlike what some MMA practitioners like to believe would happen, Miller didn't suddenly come out with all the nasty tricks and illegal techniques he knows. He didn't magically switch from using one-on-one techniques to those more suited against multiple opponents. No, he simply got beat up.

I understand this is hard to accept if you've invested a lot of time and training in MMA and you've been sold the myth that it is the best fighting system for every environment. I'm also sorry if you feel offended by my words. But that doesn't mean I'm wrong or that I'll tell a lie to make you feel better.

MMA against multiple opponents, Part 2

In the first part of "MMA against multiple opponents", a couple people left comments that bring up some interesting points. Here's one by Viro:

I think the reason sport-MMA doesn't have much of a game for a multiple-attacker scenario is that it's not an issue for those types.

The MMA folks have boiled down what works and what doesn't for the model they're working under: one vs. one in a ring with whatever particular rules exist for that venue.*

I think for MMA to come up with a vs. multiple-attacker game, there just needs to be a viable venue where someone is faced with multiple attackers. If there is enough money involved, people are going to sign up. Then we'll see MMA work to find the most efficient method to win in whatever scenario and rule-set is in place.

Oh, based on the video. I think Miller was pulling a stunt. He obviously looks jovial in the beginning of the clip. I don't think everyone/anyone else was in on it and they displayed a singular lack of humor in dealing with his shenanigans.*

*I think I read it here, but am not sure: In most leagues, you can't stomp on someone on the ground. In those leagues there is a ground game. In the leagues where you can stomp and kick someone on the ground, the person sent to the ground gets. TF. off. of. the. ground. as soon as possible.

Here are some of my thoughts in response:

- First, that was exactly my point: multiple opponents is a non-issue in MMA.
- Second, the rules indeed make the game. A small change in rules can have huge effects on the game. Remember the problems the high-kicking American kick-boxers had in the 1980's when they first faced the Dutch and French fighters who used rules that

allowed leg kicks. They were obliterated in the ring. One small change in the rules and you saw world champions get slaughtered.

- As for a multiple opponent MMA competition, there was talk about exactly such a venue. I think it was last year or the one before, not sure anymore. As far as I know, it never took off. I seriously doubt there'll ever be such a competition, a legal one that is. It comes close to manslaughter and the potential for some really nasty fixed matches is high. But it sure would be spectacular to see such a competition. I'm pretty sure it would look very different from today's UFC though…

Another comment, from Jon this time:

You raise some good points, as does Bob. The fact that the bloke was attacked in a way that didn't allow an exit skews the argument somewhat. One aspect of MMA that should be useful against multiple attackers is footwork and movement skills, but again that depends on the fighter in question.

So to the sprawl point. Some fighters sprawl just to 'sit' on someone while others sprawl to get up again immediately, even using the act of getting up to load for a knee strike or punch.

The weapon thing is an issue for sure, but covering and striking and keep on striking is one possible way of dealing with the attack, knife or not. It may not be the best or most appropriate but if it allows you an opportunity to attack that's better than nothing. But I take your point about the differences.

I suppose it's important to train for knives and multiples. I don't see that training for multiples will be detrimental to a persons MMA fighting. Machida still does his traditional karate training, admittedly not exclusively, and that hasn't stopped him becoming a champion.

I'm sure training for multiple attackers could actually enhance your one on one fighting, in terms of movement and explosive striking. I'll be interested in your views.

Here's my response:

- I don't think the "no exit" aspect was an issue because Miller never even had a chance of escaping. Look at the footage again and you'll see how quickly he gets grabbed without any possibility of escape.

- Footwork and movement is indeed a key issue with multiple attackers. But that doesn't mean the kind of footwork you see in MMA is the best for that type of situation. There are other kinds too...

- The tactical use of the sprawl does indeed vary from one fighter to the other. But the technical execution isn't all that different: for a successful sprawl, you need pretty much your entire bodyweight bearing down on the guy while you scoot your legs back. If you do this halfway, chances are you still get taken down. So in MMA, you train to do the full sprawl instinctively; I haven't seen many successful fighters who do half-sprawls and get away with it. Here's the problem: *the very act of committing your entire weight and focus on one attacker makes you vulnerable to the other attackers.* Half a second delay is enough for the others to get their hands on you. Again, look at how quickly Miller is grabbed.

- Your response on weapons is something I very much disagree with. Covering and keeping on striking against a knife is an incredibly risky strategy: the knifer doesn't need to hit you all that hard to do fatal or incapacitating damage. That's the strength of the blade; light contact can be more than enough to do some serious damage. Punching, elbowing, etc doesn't have the same potential. Look at how often MMA fighters take an insane beating before giving up or being KOed. Like Marc said: you can't trade blows against a knife; you'll lose.

- The same goes for other weapons. Try covering or shielding blocks against a tire iron... I want to see even a guy like GSP block such a blow... If he has any sense, he'll get the hell out of the way or close before the attack is launched. In both cases, the timing is very different from a typical MMA fight. You just can't soak up those blows while you wait for a shot at closing in on the guy. One hit from that tire iron (causing a broken arm, clavicle or skull) could be all it takes to break your fighting capabilities and send you to the hospital or even the morgue.

- Mind you, I'm not saying MMA **can't** work against multiple opponents. I'm saying it's dangerous and other systems are better

84

suited for the job. But these have the drawback that they suck in the Octagon. So it's a matter of choosing which one you want to learn, depending on which one you're most likely to need in your day to day life.

- As for importance, that depends. If you're into MMA, it isn't a big deal to you because you won't face weapons in the ring. Same thing for learning firearms: you won't need it in the Octagon so why train with guns? A soldier off to a war on the other hand...

- Machida is pretty much an exception to the rule. Just like Ali was one in boxing. It takes a lot of additional factors to do what Lyoto does, factors that are beyond the reach of most people. Which is why you don't see more guys fighting like him *and* be successful. Right now, Anderson Silva is the only one who comes close to being as unorthodox as Machida is.

- The reason why training for self defense (including weapons and multiple opponents)is detrimental for MMA skills is clear: it's a totally different ball game. The techniques that work best in MMA don't necessarily work as well for self defense. The tactics for MMA fights aren't geared towards defending against a thug stabbing you in the back. Like I've said ad nauseam: *the differences are just as important as the similarities.* There is overlap, yes but that isn't necessarily enough. There's overlap between Nascar and Formula 1 racing too (both use cars, both race on a track against opponents) but you don't see the best drivers from the one compete in the other. If overlap were all it took, it wouldn't be a problem to switch. But it is...

- Let's compare it to another aspect of fighting: warfare. All branches of the military use long, short and medium range weapons, they all use strategy and tactics. These are the similarities: they're all waging war, they're all fighting. But, some branches specialize in fighting on land, others in the air. Some specialize in fighting in the desert; others train specifically for the jungle or an Antarctic climate. Each specific environment requires different skills, different weapons and different tactics.

- You don't need to worry much about dehydration when you fight in a European climate. But in an Iraqi dessert, it's a real concern. How much water you can carry has a direct effect on what kind of operations you can do.

- o You don't need skis in Iraq. But on the slopes of a snow covered mountain, they're pretty frikkin' handy. Being able to march ten miles in a dessert doesn't prepare you to ski down a mountain and vice versa...
- o No matter how well you can use camouflage in the jungle, that doesn't teach you to sneak up on the enemy from under water.
- o Firing a machine gun at the enemy in a dense jungle is different from doing so in a wide, open valley. The same goes for taking cover.

- Now this is only a comparison but I think it's a valid one. Different environments/rules/situations require different skills. MMA is not self defense and vice versa. There is overlap, for sure, just like there is overlap in all the military branches and specialized units. But there are many differences and ignoring those is what gets you killed on the battlefield. Notice how I didn't say self-defense systems are "better" than MMA. Better or worse doesn't come into it. A hammer isn't better or worse than a screwdriver either. They're both nothing but tools you either use correctly or not.

For the record, I'm not having a go at Jon here. This is my personal take on things, nothing more. As always, it's your ass on the line both in the cage and on the street, so feel free to disagree with me. We all make our choices in training and do our best to make it out in one piece.

MMA against multiple opponents, Part 4

Before I start blabbering, it's easier if you read the previous parts in this "MMA against multiple opponents" series. So please do so first and then continue here.

People have misunderstood and misquoted me on these posts for a long time now, sometimes in an almost violent way. It almost seems like you're not allowed to have a nuanced discussion anymore. Newsflash: the world is not black and white. Neither is fighting. So to be clear, let me state my opinion: **MMA against multiple opponents isn't worthless. But it's also not the perfect solution for the problem.** Shades of grey, *not* black and white.

Personally, I love MMA. I think it's an awesome sport and if I were 18 right now, that's what I'd be competing in. Those days are over for me so I can't but that doesn't mean I don't appreciate the sport, on the contrary. But that also doesn't mean I drank the Kool-Aid and think MMA is the most awesome-fighting-system-EVEEEEEEEEEEER!!!!

I'm 38 as I write this and started training when I was 13. That means I narrowly missed the kung fu craze, enjoyed the ninjutsu craze when it hit, was there when silat picked up and also saw MMA rise and come into the spotlight. That's just the way the martial arts world works: every ten years or so, something "new" comes along and the audience thinks it's the best thing since sliced bread. You see this in any field, by the way, and with all kinds of products and services too.

Case in point:

My father once gave me his old mystery story magazines from the 1940s and '50s. In those, you saw adverts for... Spa treatments with radioactive material...

I am not kidding. Today, we all know now that radioactivity is not all that great for your health but back then, it was the new thing and was promoted as a being dipped in awesome-sauce, times fifty-thousand.

Today, MMA is touted as the one-stop shop for all your martial needs. Sports? Self Defense? Conditioning? Fat-loss? Penile-dysfunction? MMA solves it all (though I'm not sure about the last one...) and we have a three-disc video set on sale to show you how!

Consider how much money is involved in what has now become the MMA industry. It's billions and billions of dollars. That wasn't the case 15 years ago though, when it was looked upon as barbaric brawling by the majority of the people, including martial artists. I was there back then, I remember.

But the UFC cleaned it up by installing rounds, weight-categories and many rules to make the sport more mainstream. There's nothing wrong with that, it's what all sports do if they want to grow. But in doing so, it has strayed from the no-rules, anything goes fighting from UFC1. And even in that one you weren't allowed to bring your buddies to the fight or stab your opponent when he wasn't looking, so some perspective seems in order here.

One of the most lucrative ways of doing business in the Martial Arts today is mixing the two latest trends: MMA and Reality Based Self Defense. I think some of these programs are really good. Others are a sure way to suicide, but that's irrelevant right now. People discovered there's money to be made by combining these and that's what they're doing. As a result, it's perfect for them *if the public thinks MMA is the default way violence occurs* and they do their best to promote this agenda.

If you say otherwise, you're a traditionalist who's out of touch with reality and MMA fighters would eat you up were you to fight them... I'm only slightly joking here. I was confronted once again with this mindset just now on my blog. Here's both the comment and my reply.

Anon said:

I disagree with your analogy of this video. I believe it illustrates the necessity of grappling training for real life.

Neither of these combatants were trained in anything. This is painfully obvious, and extremely relevant. But let's pretend for a second that the guy in the white jacket was in two following scenarios. Both will be trained in either striking or grappling only. Keep in mind most BJJ guys and all MMA fighters cross train to an equal amount in both stand-up and grappling styles these days.

Scenario 1: Guy in the black jacket(BJ) is untrained but the gentleman in the white jacket(WJ) is trained in only a striking art(Karate, Boxing, Wing Chun, etc…). The fight starts and WJ starts by beating on BJ in pristine striking fashion, but is unable to avoid the clinch due to the tight space. WJ is also unable to put BJ down with strikes. Now they're in a clinching match and they go over the railing, get back up and continue wrestling. BJ takes down WJ just like in the video because WJ being primarily a striker doesn't consistently train clinching and takedown defense. Now they are both on the ground as shown in the video, and evenly matched since neither actively trains ground fighting significantly. BJ is still able to restrain WJ, and BJ's friend is still able to kick him in the head 15 times. Why? Because even though WJ is an student of striking he was ill prepared to be on the ground. In ignoring this stage of combat, he essentially wrote his own death sentence. Just because he didn't address ground combat, didn't mean he would never wind up there.

Scenario 2: Guy in the black jacket(BJ) is untrained, but this time the gentleman in the white jacket(WJ) is trained in only a grappling art(Brazilian Jiu Jitsu, Judo, Wrestling, etc…). Fight starts off as we see in the video as neither has trained striking skills to speak off. They clinch and fall over the railing still, as that would catch even the best strikers or grapplers. However they get back up as in the video and stay in the clinch. Now BJ attempts his weak takedown attempt and WJ, seeing BJ's friend, is able to keep BJ's takedown from being successful. Due to the takedown defense he regularly practices in his grappling art.

For arguments sake though lets say the fight still goes to the ground. Maybe WJ didn't see BJ's friend and took him down, maybe he got taken down and decided to stay there. We could even say they didn't get up after they tripped over the rail, as this is a major danger in any street fight, and can happen to the best fighter on the planet. Now WJ sees BJ's friend coming, and knows the ground is a terrible place to be when confronted by more than 1 person. Since he trains grappling however he is able to use his superior ground skills to reverse BJ and get back to his feet to escape. Because he knew how to fight on the ground he was able to keep from *getting pinned under BJ and escape. Something neither the real WJ nor WJ striker in scenario 1 was unable to do.*

Remember you can ignore something as hard as you want. But that doesn't mean you won't come face to face with it one day. If you don't actively train grappling, you run a risk of being taken to the ground and pinned there. Your striking skills wont help you on the ground if you lack ground experience. Essentially you become just as inexperienced as the guy who took you there, and his friends can still kick the snot out of you. Only now your inexperience makes you helpless to get back to your feet and escape.

Its like a grappler saying he didn't need to worry about getting punched because he doesn't train striking.

My reply:

Anon,

You're making things a wee bit too easy by hand picking your scenarios. There is an endless amount of different scenarios we can extrapolate from this video. You pick two that suit your bias but that doesn't make them valid in this discussion. Nor does it disqualify all other possibilities, including the ones where an MMA trained fighter gets stomped by the second guy, gets his eyes gouged out, a knife stuck in his kidneys, etc ad nauseam. I know of many real life situations where exactly this happened, and worse.

These are realities of fighting in a real life conflict, outside of the sports arena. In your words: ignore them if you will but it won't make them go away. Training for a UFC match doesn't really prepare you for that, regardless of how hard the training is.

Also, your assumptions are faulty:

Just because somebody doesn't study MMA, doesn't mean they don't study ground fighting or grappling. Grappling arts like Western wrestling or Shuai Jiao are thousands of years old. So it's safe to assume men have fought in the clinch or on the ground for a long, long time. Long before there even was a UFC.

MMA clearly admits to borrowing from those arts and adapts the techniques for fighting in the cage. That's perfectly fine. But it doesn't invalidate those original arts at all.

Nor does it mean that practitioners of these (and many, many other) arts don't train to defend against being taken down or learn how to fight on the ground. Or that their techniques and strategies are somehow inferior to MMA's.

MMA is first and foremost a sport, however rough a sport it may be. This means many things that are crucial on the street are of no consequence in the octagon. As a result, they aren't included in the training. Again, differences and similarities... That said, an MMA-trained athlete who learns all the UFC prohibited techniques and has a street-savvy mind set will be hell on wheels to fight. But he would not be welcome in the UFC anymore. And he'd also fight a lot more like what many non-MMA arts are doing.

Just two more things:

- Please look up the current position of the US Army regarding the Gracie Ju Jitsu curriculum it used: they're throwing it out. This should give you pause...
- Please talk to big city cops, soldiers on active duty in a war zone, SWAT-team members, and bouncers in rough bars (not the fancy clubs) and ask them what they prefer: training to fight on their feet or training to go to the ground and slap a triangle choke on somebody? Their response should also give you pause.

To help start the ball rolling, please read the interview I did with Mark Mireles on my blog.

He's LA's most decorated cop, has tons of real-world experience and is a MMA specialist to boot. If you think he's doesn't know what he's talking about when he says:

Ground fighting is important, but is not the absolute system for the reality of street violence. There is a place in real fighting for grappling, but most of it is for worst case scenarios, not as primary systems."

...then we'll just have to agree to disagree.

If he's not a credible source for you, then I don't know who is. My own experience and that of all my friends from the group of people I summed up above is in accord.

Respectfully,

Wim

I'm not having a go at Anon here. I just wanted to point out a mindset that is prevalent in today's MMA circles. All I can say is: to each his own. It's your life, your training, not mine. Live and let live and feel free to disagree with me.

The value of competing

In the "Karate vs. Kung Fu" post, Shane made an interesting comment I'd like to get back to now. Here's what he wrote:

Hi Wim,

Great couple of posts. I'm not sure that I agree about beating a better opponent in a competition, or losing to a worse one. If you win you are better, if you lose, you are worse. Simple as that. The competition is the empirical test, for a given set of rules at a given moment in time. We sometimes are surprised by beating or losing to someone, and occasionally luck can play a part, but if we can't use competition to gage relative ability, what can we use? Past performance? Maybe. Reputation or the color of the belt holding someone's trousers up? I sincerely hope not.

I used to enter a lot of pushing hands comps, and a few karate ones when I was younger. I mostly lost, but through perseverance gathered a handful of medals over the years. On those occasions, I dare say some of the other guys thought they should have won. If they could have, they would have, hence they were demonstrably proven wrong

I hate the 'what if' game. You know, if I had just done this technique, I would have won for sure. If I was more mentally prepared. If I had lost a few pounds and gone down a weight. (Or in my case, if I had just spent less time sitting on my arse drinking beer, and more time doing nei kung) It's all fantasy, and competitions are the corresponding reality check.

All the best,

Shane

Here's how I see it:

For me, it's not really a "What if?" game. There's certainly a place for that as analyzing your performance after the fight is key to improving your abilities. But I'm not all that concerned about what I *should* have done. I'm usually thinking more about getting it right the next time. Fights are chaos in action and there's just no way you'll get it right every single time. But that doesn't mean you shouldn't try.

By playing a constructive "What if" game, you use the experience from losing a fight to your advantage. Instead of beating yourself up over what you did wrong, you get over it and focus on how to avoid making the same mistake. Of course, there is rarely a black and white solution for whatever mistakes you made. Usually, there are a bunch of options you could have tried, each with varying chances of success. I think that's just wicked cool. It means more learning during training and I enjoy that the most. But I digress, back on track:

For me, the value of competing lies in several aspects:

- You train harder than usual when you're in preparation for a fight. As a result, you learn more about your art, you get in better shape and increase your skills.
- You're forced to look at yourself in an honest way: which techniques am I good at? Which ones do I suck at? In other words: what is good, what is bad and how do I improve upon the former while fixing the latter.
- If you lie to yourself about those things, you'll pay for it. So you better be honest.
- You have to overcome your own fears and demons. They all come out to play both in training and during the fight.
- It's just pure, uncensored, Neanderthal fun.

I also said in that post that I lost to fighters who were not as good as me. By that I mostly mean that I was stronger, in better shape and/or more skilled than them. But I still lost because I wasn't focused enough or didn't handle the pre-fight stress correctly. Putting it differently, had there been no crowds, just the two of us in a ring, I'm confident I would have done much better. I'm not bitter about those lost fights, I did what I could and there's not much more I could have done.

Another aspect to competing is how it's just a snapshot in time of your and your opponent's abilities: Take on the same guy a month earlier or later and the results could be reversed. If you lose to a guy now and then train with a vengeance, you might beat him easily a year or two later. Or he might beat you once again, who knows? Every sport has great rivalries where competitors are too evenly matched for one of them to beat the other consistently.

So in the end, it doesn't mean all that much if you win or lose. There is always somebody better than you. There are also always many who are loads worse too. Sooner or later, you'll be too old to keep up with the younger generation. But if you fight those younger guys without rules, things like experience and being a mean old SOB can turn the tide in your favor. Which is why I don't think competitions have much actual value as a benchmark for real world performance. It's better than nothing, but certainly not the be all, end all.

Respect in the Mixed Martial Arts

This post is inspired by a YouTube clip by Erik Paulson in which he talks a little about respect in NHB and MMA. Look for the video titled "Erik Paulson – Respect"

I couldn't agree more with everything he said, especially about the getting old part. I'm only a few years younger than Eric but feel the same way: I used to be part of the young generation and now I'm one of the "old guys."

By the way, one of the ways I first noticed this was when my younger students weren't getting some of my jokes anymore. For instance, when one of them moved their head first and then turned their body, I told him *"Don't move like RoboCop"* and then showed what they did wrong. Most students understood right away what I was talking about. Now, they just look at me with a slightly confused look on their face and say "Robo-what?"

Eventually I looked it up and it turns out the movie came out well over 20 years ago, way before they were even born. Proof positive I'm getting old... Anyway, back to the respect thing.

I noticed the same thing Erik did:

When I started training, the teacher's word was law and you did what he said, period. You didn't question him, you didn't talk to him like he was one of the other students, none of that. I would never have dreamed of interrupting my teacher or asking questions while he was busy with somebody else. You just didn't do that. Today, I have students yelling for me from across the room...

Up to a point, this is normal. Society always changes and social conventions change along with it. So it's only normal today's youngsters are different from when I was their age. But I still make them do the palm/fist salute at the beginning and end of class. And also when they start and stop working with a training partner. Simply becausethere are compelling reasons to keep giving them a sense of respect during the training. There are many more but to make sense for the typical MMA-testosterone loudmouth **(*)** , I'll limit myself to these here:

- **Becoming a *good* fighter is about self-discipline**, doing what you *need* to do instead of what you *want* to do: You might *want* to spar weaker opponents all the time because it's fun but to make progress, you'll *have* to work with stronger ones. Not so much fun when you eat leather all the time, but it's necessary to improve your skills.

- **Respect is also all about self-discipline.** It's about restraining your own feelings, desires, little (or big) pet peeves and hold all that back while you concentrate on someone other than yourself: your teacher, your fellow students, your opponents, the rest of the world basically. If you can't even control yourself enough to show respect to these people, you probably won't have the discipline to excel in the ring, cage or on the lei tai.

- **Becoming a *smart* fighter is about seeing the strength and weakness of others.** You have to respect those strengths and try to use their weakness against them. To do that, you have to get out of your own head, forget your ego and admit that some opponents will be better than you. Maybe not in every aspect of the fight game but it will happen eventually. This doesn't mean you can't beat them, but you will have to analyze them honestly and correctly first.

- **Respect is *also* about seeing the strength and weakness in yourself.** If you don't respect your opponents, if you think they're all bums and losers, how will you make an accurate, dispassionate assessment of your own skills? You can't; you'll just assume you're better than them regardless of the evidence to the contrary staring you in the face. As a result, you'll (subconsciously) underestimate their strong points and overestimate your weaknesses. Which is a sure fire way to lose any fight against them.

Here's the kicker: *You can't fake respect.* You can go through the motions and fool other people but never yourself. In your little, dark heart, you **know** how you *really* feel about other fighters or fellow students. Which brings you right back to the problems I listed in the list here above:

- Lack of respect/self-discipline breeds sloppy, lazy fighters.
- It also creates illusions of grandeur in your own head.

Saluting your teacher, bowing to your opponent, touching gloves, it all serves as a constant reminder that you need to work hard and never think you've arrived. Because slacking off means your opponent has more time to train harder than you, get better and eventually beat you. And that includes the other students in class, even those you might not like or don't enjoy training with.

The reality of combat sports is that fights are always snapshots in time: Today you win, next time you might lose against the same guy. You might dominate him today and next time, he knocks you out with a lucky shot. Anything can and will happen when two fighters go at each other. That's just how it works. To avoid Mr. Murphy determining the outcome of your fights, you have to do everything in your power to be better, stronger, faster, more technical, smarter, etc. than the other guy.

The only way you can do that is with *loads ofself-discipline*. Respect is simply another aspect of that.

(*****) Yes, yes, I know not every fighter is a loudmouth-asshole. I'm just making a point, don't take it personally OK? I'm talking about Tito Ortiz disrespecting Mark Coleman after he lost to Randy Couture, Brock Lesnar's tirade after he beat Frank Mir, that kind of thing.

Respect in the Mixed Martial Arts, Part 2

In the previous part of "Respect in the Mixed Martial Arts", I focused mainly on the negative side, the lack of respect many MMA fighters show and why it hurts their progress. But there are many more reasons why giving respect, bowing and saluting are important. Here are some of them:

- **Safety.** When you train full contact, there's always the chance of something going wrong because fighting is inherently dangerous. In training, you sometimes need to crank up the intensity but the goal is simulating your upcoming fight and not injuring your sparring partners. Bowing or saluting both before and after each round/exercise/whatever is a way to avoid those injuries. It clearly defines when you can both *start* throwing techniques and when you both agree to *stop*. This makes it a powerful safety protocol. Think of it like wearing your seat belt in a car or a helmet when you walk around on a construction site: it doesn't mean nothing can happen to you; it means the odds of you getting seriously injured go down a bit.

- **Keep your ego in check.** This relates to the previous bullet: when you train with hard contact, tempers easily flare. You might think the other guy is hitting way too hard for the drill you're doing or he might think you're messing it up on purpose and are trying to hurt him. Either way, it's easy to get caught up in the moment, crank it up a notch and turn things into a real fight.Touching gloves or bowing before you begin reminds you why you're there: to learn and increase your skill. Both goals require you to keep your ego in check. Showing respect helps you do just that and allows you to train better.

- **Focus.** A key component of winning a fight is your mindset. Even if you're the strongest, fastest guy around, you can still lose if your head isn't screwed on right. Your ability to focus is therefore one of the most important skills you have to train. A practical and easy way to do that is saluting your training partner at the beginning

99

and end of the round/drill. You can make the physical act of touching gloves, slapping a high five or bowing your head a powerful mental trigger. One that helps you focus entirely on the task at hand and drive out all other thoughts, worries or concerns: as you salute, you narrow the world down to just you and your partner. As with all worthwhile skills, you need to train hard before this actually works. Saluting or bowing every time gives you plenty of opportunity to practice…

- **It keeps you human.** I know this might sound weird, but bear with me. Non-team sport athletes are some of the most egocentric people in the world; I know because I used to be one. When you compete, everything is about *you*: *your* training, *your* upcoming fight, *your* season, *your* recuperation, *you*, *you*, *you*. Living like that for years on end can easily turn you into a selfish bastard, one who uses his career and fights as an excuse to do as he pleases in all other aspects of his life and subsequently treats his loved ones unfairly. I wasn't as bad as some guys I knew but, I do speak from bitter experience. You become so used to everything being organized around your person that you take it for granted. Do it long enough and you eventually turn into an asshole. I don't know about you, but I don't want to be a flaming asshole (*"Too late!"* some people will say…) Showing respect to other fighters and your trainer is a way to stay humble and human. It reminds you you're not the only one who matters in this world.

There are even more reasons than that but I don't want to dwell on it; you get the point.

Before I go on, some more thoughts:

- This is always work in progress. We're all only human. But that doesn't mean you shouldn't try.
- MMA has become so big it pays to be a "bad boy". Bad boy = media attention = bigger pay day. Tito Ortiz made a career out of it but like Eric said, in person he's not like that. In other sports, you see this too when competitors make themselves hot property for the media by acting all wild to increase their marketability. If you look at the merchandising and marketing contracts they act

that way, you'll see why some take that route. Not every fighter does so, but it sure works in getting more money coming your way.

Here's an examples of how you don't have to be a low-life to be a great fighter:

Musashi was never the greatest fighter in the K1 circuit. In fact, he had almost as many losses as he had wins. But he stuck it out for 14 years even though he got KOed numerous times, including by Lebanner. In his retirement fight, he fought better than he had in a long time and wasn't afraid to take the fight to his opponent, Jerome Lebanner. Even though he won, Lebanner showed tremendous respect after the fight by kneeling into seiza and bowing before Musashi to honor the Japanese fighter for his career and the warrior spirit he showed in their last fight. Musashi clearly became extremely emotional then.

There are many more such examples so don't go thinking all fighters are a bunch of thugs. Some are, some aren't.

The question is, do *you* want to be known as one or not?

"Don't be a knucklehead"

Look up the video called "Keith Owen on: Grappling the "Anti You"" on YouTube. I learned about this clip via a mailing list I'm on and want to give mad props to Mr. Owen. First, listen to what he says: "Don't be a knucklehead".

Isn't that the truth? At every stage in your training, there is one consistent factor: the need for technical training. It doesn't matter if you're a rank beginner or have been training for decades; you always have to focus on increasing both your technical knowledge and skill.

Why?

Because there is no alternative as one day, you won't have anything else left to make the magic work.

Strength fades as you get older, speed goes away as well, anaerobic conditioning will become increasingly harder to do and so it goes on. But technical skills and experience only continue to grow. The one caveatis that you have to maintain a minimum of physical training to access techniques. Technique can compensate for a lot of deficiencies but there is a physical threshold you have to pass or it won't work: If your body is as solid as a wet noodle, that Neanderthal brute who's pissed at you for "stealing" his parking space will blast through your exquisite technique anyway. So there are minimum physical requirements you can't ignore.

However, I'm not saying you can neglect your physical attributes when you reach a higher skill level. Technique can certainly trump raw force but what if you can *also* maintain your speed and strength to the highest level at whatever age you are? Wouldn't that trump *only* having loads of skill?

I certainly think so. That's why I still do my conditioning as much as possible: Tabata protocol training, bodyweight exercises, etc. I do less than in the past but I still lift iron occasionally, along with speed work and everything else I can think off. I want to stack the cards in my favor as much as I can, for as long as I can.

My guess is that it takes a while before most practitioners figure out the importance of technical skills and how there's no real limit to them. Many beginning students fall in love with training hard and rough. I agree that it's fun and it has immense value but there are also limits to it. If, as Mr. Owen says, you go 100% all of the time, you end up hurt all the time too. You'll also lose training partners/students to injuries and burn out: very few people like to be in pain or get beat up all the time.

But what's more, it slows down your progress. The 100%-mode doesn't allow for much experimenting or creativity. Nor does it let you iron out small (or big) errors in your techniques because you're too busy trying to win or beat the other guy. It becomes too much a result-oriented approach (beat him) and no longer process-driven (do the techniques correctly). For best results, you need both. You need to go after your opponent with the will to beat him. But you'll achieve that faster and easier the better your technical skills are. So it's a trade-off.
I'm a firm believer in training hard and sparring hard. But there's no need to do that all the time. Sparring is *synthesis*, where you put all the pieces together to the best of your abilities. Training is *analysis*, where you look at each individual piece and polish it. After the sparring, you go back to perfecting and polishing the attributes that went wrong or could have been better during sparring.

You need both but not in the same amounts if you want to train for the rest of your life. As a teacher, you need to make your students understand the importance of both and the differences between them. Case in point:

In one of my classes, we sparred for 20 min. at the end. It wasn't an all-out session, just technical sparring. One of my newer students (about 1 year of training) has a habit of cranking it up when he gets hit. This isn't a bad thing per se; I prefer a student's fighting spirit to rouse when he gets hit over cowering or giving up. But that surge of energy needs to be controlled and he never managed that before. As he was getting better and tougher, I took him up on it this time:

I tagged him with a punch and he reacted with a full power kick, which I blocked. The kick was much harder than anything he'd thrown before. His leg wasn't even back on the floor when my on kick slammed into his stomach. He dropped and sucked air for a while. Now I hadn't hit him full power (I never do with my students) but it was harder than I have ever hit him before.

I then explained to him how his fighting spirit is letting him get carried away when he's tagged. Which results in a telegraphed kick and an easy job for me to counter him. But more importantly, he no longer pays attention to what his opponent is doing because he becomes too focused on hitting hard. I was also not at the ideal distance for the kick he threw and he neglected to turn his hip correctly, giving mine a clear path to his stomach. It was easy for me to exploit all that and counter successfully.

He understood that and then I told him that in the next sparring session, he can work on taking a step back when he gets hit. That step allows him to think about his next move instead of running into a counter.

There's nothing wrong with training at 100% intensity. You'll learn loads of important things. But it's just another tool in your toolbox and not the ultimate one.

Advice, wasted on the young

I was teaching class this week and found myself unable to completely get certain things across to my students:

- Why you need to turn your hip completely into that kick, even if you hit plenty hard without it.
- Why you should always come back to the on guard position in training.
- Why hitting hard is not the most important thing and pursuing only that limits your other skills.
- Why it's vital they follow procedure when training and not get creative before they have more experience.

The list goes on and on. Each of those points requires a long explanation to do it justice when they ask "Why?" But class is not the place for that. So as a teacher, I try to condense the most important elements to answer the question and still get the point across. But that inevitably leaves out so much. And too often, the student still doesn't get it.

How do I know? When I spot him doing the exact same error five minutes later instead of practicing what I explicitly told him to do. Not all students are that way but many are. It isn't "fun" to drill in a correction until the error goes away. Sparring and hitting the bag is cooler. But it's through that errorthat they'll get tagged by the opponent who spots it. And then all the other cool stuff will be useless.

It isn't as simple as that, but I'm making it simple to get the point across: many times, you're better off just doing what the teacher says instead of asking an explanation. Not always, obviously. But most often, you need to follow the advice and not ignore it or simply gloss over it.

I'm not a big fan of the old Chinese teaching method of "Shut up and do it because I tell you to" but it does offer some benefits in this specific area. If a teacher gave you advice on how to do things, you did it until he said otherwise. This is a powerful teaching method. Flawed, potentially dangerous, but it works. Here's a good example, from my failing memory so don't sue me if I get the details wrong:

Japanese martial artist and researcher Kenji Tokitsu once wrote about how one of his sword teachers told him to hit a car tire with his wooden practice sword, 500 times each day. And so he did, for years on end. His teacher never asked about or mentioned the exercise again though. So after several years, Kenji stopped doing that exercise, figuring it was useless or that his teacher had forgotten about it. The next time he saw his teacher, they had just started training when the old man asked "Have you stopped practicing on the tire?" Kenji had to admit he had done exactly that. With any further training apparently useless, his teacher ended the class right there and told him to resume practicing on the tire.

I always liked that story, even though I thought it was exaggerated when I read it twenty years ago. Today, I can honestly say I get it. I'm no grand master or anything like that, but I can tell when students practice the exercises I advised them to do at home. The same goes for those who didn't.

Anyway, this rambling came about after Thursday's class combined with hearing the Baz Luhrmann song "Everybody's Free (To Wear Sunscreen)" again yesterday. It's a great tune, with loads of great advice that is all too often wasted on the young. I guess the same is true in martial arts classes.

Some thoughts on my own training

When I started training in my early teens, I thought I was hot stuff because we trained hard in my old Kung Fu school. Then I got my butt kicked by muay Thai guys. Back to the drawing board to learn what they know. Once I could hold my own there, those nasty South-East Asian guys got through with their funky techniques and left me gasping in pain. Once again, time to learn their way. Then I got put on my butt as if I were a sick, little child by tai chi players. And so the story goes on and on.

Obviously, I don't train in every style out there because there are only 24 hours in a day. But if I could, I would. That said, there are striking similarities between styles and the trick in handling them is not learning the same thing twice: The differences between kickboxing and muay Thai are smaller than those between judo and harimau silat. Once you start seeing the differences and similarities, it becomes a bit easier. Of course, knowing a solution and implementing it is not the same thing. You still have to train hard to have a shot at pulling it off. Which is why I train in as many arts as I can, with certain limitations: Sports fighting becomes less important as I get older.

I'm not going to compete anymore so there's little point in focusing all my time on those arts. They have immense value but also a bunch of limitations you don't find in traditional arts. By training both, I feel I get the best of everything and am a better fighter for it:

- I may not be the best Tai Chi player out there but I'm a better Sanshou fighter than most of them.
- I may not be the best Sanshou fighter but I'm a better Silat player than most of them.
- I may not be the best Silat player out there but I'm a better muay Thai fighter than most of them.

In case you missed it, I **didn't** say I was the best in any one of those arts and everybody else sucks. I am saying I *try* to be more versatile than people who train in just one art or in a bunch of arts from the same family. So far, I feel this has given me far more benefits than drawbacks. To each his own and you have to live with the consequences of your choices. I'm OK with mine.

Some more thoughts on my own training

In the previous post, I mentioned some of my views on training and there was some good stuff in the comments section.

John said:

I think in the end, that's all any of us can hope for… there is always someone better out there but at least for me – the competition is with myself. You know – self-improvement/enlightenment.

I believe this is one of the keys to make it through the difficult patches when you train your entire life. When I was younger, I competed a lot and it was tons of fun. Beating opponents always felt great, obviously. But for me, the training and preparation was the most fun of all. Every day, you have to push yourself to be faster, better, stronger. I learned so much just by training for my fights, I doubt I'd know half of what I know now if I hadn't done that.

But there's another side to this coin: training is fun, winning is awesome, but losing is the most important lesson of all. I lost to guys who were way better than me. They cleaned my clock. I won fights against less skilled opponents as well as against better ones. But most importantly, I lost fights against guys I could have beaten easily, if my head had been screwed on right. I learned important lessons from those losses. They taught me to place things in the proper context and how fighting is rarely black and white, one side being "better" than the other.

Fast forward another decade or so and things have changed again. These days, it's no longer relevant where I rank in that subjective hierarchy of who is "better" than me in any given art. Or who is the best fighter. Like I said before, there are loads of people with more skill than me. There are also a truckload of others with less skill. Sometimes the differences are really big, other times not so much.

Who cares? What does it matter?

Somebody else's (lack of) skill doesn't change anything about my own. If he has less, I don't automatically get any extra. If he has more, I don't automatically lose some. It just is what it is: a momentary assessment of somebody's qualities. A year later, the assessment might be just the opposite, so why worry about it now? It doesn't mean that I'd automatically beat the guy with lesser skill if we were to fight. Nor does it mean the one with more skill has nothing to worry about if we were to go at it.

Fighting, by its very nature, is never done in a static environment. There are many variables and skill is just one of them. An important one, but not to the exclusion of all the others. That said, when everything comes together, it can be awesome. Case in point:

The first time I entered a pushing hands competition was many years ago. My teacher and I went to the Dutch Open and he gave me some basic strategy to follow. I applied it to one of my first opponents and broke his balance easily to score a point. I figured, what the hell, so I did the same thing again with the same result: the other guy falls, I get points. After about the fifth or sixth time, I start thinking "He's setting me up. Where's the trap? " but still I kept scoring with the exact same technique. At the end of the match, it was something like 30-0 in my favor and the guy looked really frustrated. That's when I realized he really didn't know what to do against my attack. Even knowing full well what was coming, he couldn't handle it.

Sometimes, the "magic" works and it's a great feeling.

Finally, here's a comment from Mark:

Also, versatility, cross training, keeping an open mind etc. These are all phrases that complement every martial artist and can do nothing but GOOD for their fighting. It is not uncommon for an expert fighter to train in another style and get dominated. It is best to train with as many styles as possible, as all knowledge gained will be useful. Having said that, I do feel that it is wise to stick to one style only for a few years to grasp the basic principles of movement, body usage etc, if you are just starting out. This would also help you pick up other styles easier later on.

Mark touches upon one of the major problems today's novice martial artists encounter: there's too much choice.

When I started, we had a couple of schools in a variety of arts where we could train. There were books and some videotapes you could use to see how other arts worked if you couldn't go train elsewhere. When my own teachers started, there were just some books and that was it. If you couldn't find somebody to train with, you didn't learn anything. Period.

Today, martial art schools and gyms pop up like mushrooms. They're all over the place and give you the widest possible range of arts to practice. Even some of the more obscure arts are now almost always available in a gym near you. If they're not, you can buy videos from the country of origin or watch clips on the Internet. Putting it mildly: there has never been so much information available.

But perhaps because of that, many practitioners change arts like they change clothes. If there's something they don't like about it, they pick another one. If that one has some lame things in it, they're off again. And so on.

If there's one drawback to all the benefits of an abundance of information, it's this tendency to propagate shallow knowledge. Just because you spent three years in a style, it doesn't mean you know everything there is about it. Nor are you in a position to correct people with decades of training. Even more, you certainly don't have any reason to assume that what you learned is universally true for all other styles or even different branches of your own.

This really shows in some of the comments I get on my YouTube channel but it's not just my stuff: pretty much everybody who puts a video online gets a fair amount of misguided, or at worst, vile and idiotic comments. Like I mentioned before, I'm perfectly fine with what I can and can't do. Nor do I present anything I teach as the "Ultimate-Unbeatable-Betterthaneverythingelse"- whatever. But that doesn't stop people from writing the silliest things in the comments section.

Sometimes, it cracks me up. I've literally laughed so hard I started crying over some comments. Other times, I shake my head at the bile my "pygmy detractors" (as one of my teachers calls them) spew. For the most part, I try to give a respectful and clear response. Other times, I respond with humor because I don't take their insults seriously: keyboard warriors are to be pitied because their lives are already hard enough.

I'm guessing a lot of those comments are fueled by a lack of training and understanding. Three years in a style is nothing. Ten years is just enough to get you started. Twenty years is when it starts getting interesting. I'll let you know what happens after thirty years when I get there. But I've heard some neat things about it...

So I totally agree with Mark: cross-training has huge benefits. But you need a stable base first.

From my mailbox

Over the years, I've gotten all sorts of mail. Some good, some bad. Some flattering as hell, some cursing at me like a sailor in desperate need for shore leave. And also everything in between those extremes. With broadband becoming common place, YouTube and forums taking over the world, it seems everybody has an opinion (however misinformed it may be) and absolutely **has** to share it. If I write something they don't like, they start spouting bile via e-mail.

Nowadays, I don't respond to hate mail anymore. Thanks to technological advances, it automatically gets transferred to a special folder where it gets logged for future reference. But when I started my first site over ten years ago, I took the time to reply to everybody, regardless of how rude they were.

Here's an example:

Your review of his book was not accurate. You have a very "know it all attitude". Your lack of knowledge and discipline to the art was obvious. It is scary and depressing that an aspiring student could be misled by your comments. Also, it appears you have applied some of the techniques in experimental fashion while sparring. Your martial arts experience and friendship with a doctordid not prepare you to understand Master Long's book. As for driving someone's nose up into their brain, it is a 2 move technique.It is very obvious that youlack the maturity toaccurately evaluate texts such as Long's. Please re-read the book and amend your review.

My response:

Hi,

I notice you don't really like the review, an opinion to which you are obviously entitled. But it is a bit difficult to comment on your mail because you do not identify yourself. Do you know Hei Long? Have you studied with him? If so, how long? Basically, what makes you qualified to criticize my review? For all I know, you might be a 14-year old having fun with e-mail.

All the best,

Wim

His reply:

Hello,

I owe you an apology for the scathing review. Your response was very politecompared to myinitial appraisal. I am not a medical doctor. I am achiropractor (now ten years in practice). My education took ten years of college specialized in the neuromusculoskeletal system. As this material was rather dry, I wouldalso studybooks such as master Long's and Dim Mak. I've always held an interest in martial arts but have never struck another person; it is not my nature. However, my job requires moving articulations in a precise direction, with specific depth, speed and force – very similar to the martial arts. In studyingmaster Long'sbook, I understood the mechanisms and their application. I do not doubt the effectiveness of these strikes if executed correctly.I wish you well in your studies.If you know of interesting texts, please let me know.

More often than not, I got a similar response when people realize they were mouthing off. Sometimes it only makes things worse though. This one here was the last response in a series by some nutcase:

Your end will be damnation if you don't repent to Christ you demented antichrist propagandist.

Yup, that's me, the antichrist propagandist…

Then there's the mail I get with a certain type of question… How about this:

*The Fila Brasileiro Association wishes to invite Jerome LeBanner to be a FBA Delegate in France. Please ask him to contact Mrs. *******, the FBA Secretary in **********. Thanks.*

Errr... How am I supposed to know JLB? I only did a review of his video, that's it!

This one here was also a bit special:

Hello Dim

I have visited your website and enjoyed viewing the video clips, great combinations and techniques.

As you have been the national coach to the belgium you certainly know about iranian san shou fighters.

It will be my honor and pleasure to cooperate with you in various fields related to martial arts.I have moved for permanent residnce to ************.

Iwill send you articles and also video clips in the near future and hope you find them interesting and useful,your ones were absolutely useful for me and I will train them.

I invite you to visit my website and take a look at page "About US" to become more familliar with each other.The website address is: ******************

Do you want to know what are the most important lessons,I have learned in martial arts:

"There is always something new to learn' and "Never get selfish cos there is always someone better than you"

Looking forward to hear from you friend,I have made many friends all over the world,but you are my first one in Belgium.

I wish you merry christmas.

Kindest Regards

Friend ********

Imagine getting that one out of the blue... First of all, I'll pick my own friends, thank you very much. Second, if you start off by calling me "Dim" instead of getting my first name right, you're probably not going to make it to the friend zone…

Then there are the freebie searchers:

i would like a kick boxing inst tape i would like to get into kick boxing could u help me out thank you *******

or this little gem:

dear sirs i like to learn your style but i have no money would a book help me out please right back any advise for me

No worries, I'll send you a couple thousand dollars worth of instructional material right away! Just because you asked! Shees…

This is just a sample of the funniest ones but I get loads more mail in the same vein. Just to be clear, I don't mind people contacting me, not at all. I do mind:

- Rudeness. I don't need to take abuse.
- Freebie seekers. Why on earth do people expect me to send them free books and videos, make them a personalized training schedule, etc. Just because I have a website? You want something? Buy it like everybody else. If I walk into a bakery and ask for a free loaf of bread, they'll laugh or call the police. Why would I do any different?
- Time wasters: Reading my blog doesn't entitle anybody to my time. No, I'm not going to search for Remy Bonjasky's telephone number for you. No, I'm not going to look for a Tae Bo club for you in Amsterdam. And the list goes on and on. You want it, do it yourself.

I didn't used to be like this though. I used to try and help people but rarely got even a "Thank you." mail back from them. So I eventually got tired of doing all the work for those people and now no longer reply.

You notice I was kind enough to obscure the names and other identifiers from the mails (though I left their typos intact…). I have that information of course, but there's no need to plaster it all over these pages. You know who you are…

Martial Intent, the wrong way

After the "Crazy Monkey kung fu" post, several people commented on how weird it looked. And also how this type of "go nuts and flip out" fighting might surprise you at first. Let's look at the last part first.

One of the fighting "temperaments" is just that: *you flip out and go crazy, making you very unpredictable.*

It's very surprising the first time you fight somebody like that. Unless you have lots of experience, you might get caught by a sucker punch from such an opponent because of his antics. You see guys like this on the street for different reasons:

- They're pumping themselves up while at the same time trying to intimidate you.
- It just happens to be their preferred way fighting.
- They're crazy, as in certifiably so.
- A combination of the above.

When you're faced with such a person, it can go bad for you because of that unpredictable way of fighting. You don't have to lie down and start bleeding just yet, but there's definitely an extra difficulty to handling these guys if you haven't faced them before. My personal preferences to tackle them:

- If they're not attacking you just yet but are flipping out, leave ASAP. If you can't, strike first, fast and hard. It's difficult to jump up and down and be all hyper-active when your knee is busted or your cracked ribs are sticking out...
- If they're coming at you, you might like to:
  - o Side step quickly and counter very, very hard.
  - o Fire a powerful long range technique as they come in (balance is not their strong point) but only if you know you

have the speed, power and timing to do the job of stopping them cold.
o Grab a tool (preferably a big one) and hit them with it.

Obviously, anything can go wrong but in my experience, these guys are usually not prepared for an immediate and powerful response from somebody who they see as a victim. I find the right mindset for this to be:

"I don't care how crazy you are; I'll just hit you really, really hard right now."

The first question remains though: *why on earth would somebody train weird stuff like those guys in the video?*

For a variety of reasons actually. I covered the tactical surprise here above but there's more.

By now, everybody knows about the need for adrenal stress conditioning for effective self-defense. We've been fortunate that a lot of research became available in the last few decades, giving us the scientific framework to understand the psychological and physiological reasons for this.

But a couple hundred years ago, this knowledge didn't exist. Nobody knew what adrenaline was, nor why the human brain reacts the way it does when you're faced with violence or mortal combat. But that didn't stop people from fighting and waging war. So they had to find ways to cope with the fear, weak knees and other undesirable responses to adrenal stress.

Going apeshit like these guys do is one of the ways to do that.

Think of the last time you were so pissed-off, angry as hell and ready to rip somebody's head off. If somebody puts an aggressive opponent in front of you right then and there, you're about as ready to fight as you'll ever be. Chances are actually pretty good he'll back down from the fight when he sees the look in your eyes.

I'm not saying it's the best way but there are similar practices in many tribal and warrior societies. And for good reason because this approach really works. The easier it is for you to get this worked up, the less reserve you'll have to hurt the guy in front of you. In fact, you'll be itching to cut loose. As a basic self defense mind-set, this is a good place to start:

- Somebody is about to attack you.
- A second later, you're loaded up on adrenaline and your whole body goes into "Fight"-mode.
- You're also immediately extremely pissed off and ready to mutilate the guy.

If you can manage that, your odds of surviving the attack improve big time. Which might have you thinking *"Wicked cool! I'm in!"*
Perhaps you shouldn't go down that road just yet though. There are several reasons why this kind of training is a bad idea. First, because it looks stupid in training. I mean, just look at those Chinese guys… But there's more:

- It takes a lot out of you, even in training. It's draining both physically and emotionally.
- If you do it too long or too much, it alters your character and invites in a host of psychological problems.
- Those problems will eventually force you to make some bad decisions and create a nightmare of a life for you.

But the most important reason is this: *it's a beginner's way to get ready for a fight.*

Yes, you flood your system with adrenaline and it gears up for a fight in a heartbeat.

Yes, your mind-set is all about battle.

But unless you have loads of experience, almost all of your technical, tactical and strategic skills will be gone. You'll resort to fighting on a primitive level, caveman style, hopefully hitting hard and fast enough so the other guy doesn't have time to do damage.

As you're overcome by that battle-rage, *you don't have mental energy left to see what the other guy is doing, which leaves you wide open.* And you won't even *know* your defense has holes in it big enough to drive a truck through. Until it's too late that is...

I've had people go nuts on me several times. Invariably, I nailed them with the tactics I explained earlier. The main reasons I could do so was exactly that: a total lack of defense. Their whole game is based on being more aggressive and offensive than you. Take that away from them and there's not much left. Mind you, if they can nail you with one of their wild attacks, you'll be in trouble. But if you can get your own power shot in first, the odds are good they won't be able to defend against it.

What's better then?

There are many different ways of building up your fighting mind-set, too many to mention here so I'll quickly point you to some resources:

- Read the post about "Martial Intent" and watch the clips of the Blacks doing their thing. The Haka is one of those traditional ways of preparing for battle. See how they gear up both mind and body to fight, *but stay in total control of themselves.*
- I wrote a chapter in Loren W. Christensen's book "Solo Training 2" about creating mental triggers. It covers the basics of mental programming for both self defense and combat sports.
- Loren also just released a great book called "Warrior Mindset" that'll give you plenty of insight too.

This information will help you get started but let me tell you upfront: there are no shortcuts. Some people naturally have a good fighting mind-set or it came to them after years of living in a dangerous place. Or they've been doing a high-risk job for so long, it's just a part of them.

If that's not you, you'll have to work hard and for a long time to get to a point where you can program your mind effectively. And it's rarely a fun thing to do. It's one of the areas of martial arts and self defense where "The Dark Side" is waiting for you. Or you might not like what you discover about yourself in the process. Which is why I always caution students when they ask me about this. Caveat emptor.

25 Questions

Here's a fun one: Kris Wilder asked me to join up for this new site he started. The concept is pretty simple: different people get to write 25 things; questions, statements, it doesn't matter. If you like that sort of thing, here's my list.

25. I never know how to start lists like this. It's always a balance between giving too much personal information and not saying anything worth reading.

24. When I was a teenager, I often pretended to have cerebral palsy while I waited for the train. It taught me how fundamentally evil people can be towards their fellow man: they avoided me like the plague, were vicious and rude, got up and left when I sat next to them, etc.

23. I have five first names. Don't ask...

22. If I could, I'd train all day long, every day of the year.

21. Sometimes I still feel like the shy boy I was thirty years ago. But for some reason, nobody believes that's true. Go figure...

20. Every now and then, I think practicing martial arts is pretty vacant. What kind of weirdo spends all his time finding better ways to kill, maim and hurt other people?

19. Then I remember the countless benefits of practicing and train a bit harder.

18. In my bedroom is a framed quote of something James Joyce wrote to his wife. It's the most accurate expression of true love I've ever read. The woman who wakes up next to me in the morning gets to read it every time because it expresses perfectly how I feel about her.

17. I love vampire books and movies. Just love 'em.

16. I've been accused of thinking too much by more than one person. They're probably right.

15. I'm the biggest IT nerd and gadget freak I know.

14. I used to be so convinced I was right about so many things. Then I learned I was wrong. These days, I tend to think I might be on to something but everybody else probably figured it out already.

13. Whenever I feel bad about a situation and can't fix it, I remember my mother's advice on those things. It's not something I can repeat in public...

12. Sometimes, when I look at my children, I wish my own father had lived longer.

11. I can't imagine life without books. You can keep your E-readers, I want to turn pages and find out what's behind the next one.

10. I wish I could sing or play an instrument well. My children wish it even more when I break into song and clouds gather for a storm.

9. One of my best memories: standing on top of a hill in Phoenix, Arizona. Two dear friends by my side, watching the sun set. I was in a bad place then but being there made it all go away for a little while. Priceless.

8. I could listen to Pavarotti sing Nessun Dorma all day long. Even though Turandot isn't that good an opera.

7. Why is it that every time I'm in a hurry, a slow-moving truck is in front of me and there's no chance of passing it?

6. If I could, I'd travel constantly to spend more time with friends in different countries all over the world.

5. Teaching is my greatest passion. It fulfills me in ways nothing else can.

4. Writing is a close second. Nothing compares to finishing a manuscript and sending it off to the publisher. Perhaps the feeling of picking up a published book for the first time...

3. My plan is to train and teach until I die. Or until my wheelchair breaks down. We'll see which comes first...

2. I've been blessed to have met and become friends with some amazing people.

1. I love my children and partner more than words can express, more than they'll ever know. The sun rises and sets with them.

The art in martial arts

Yesterday, I talked to somebody about an item on my 25 questions list. He hated opera and couldn't understand why I enjoyed listening to some fat guy shouting incomprehensible words at the top of his lungs... Straying a bit from my usual posts on martial arts, here's some more on that.

I tried to explain to him that:

- **I like all kinds of music:** I listen to anything from Entombed and Slayer to whatever is playing in the charts. Rap, Latin music, you name it, I like it. Opera is just another one on a long list of musical genres I enjoy. Though, for the record, I hate (most) country and (all) reggae music with a vengeance. Keep your "Yah man!" crap and smoke it...
- **Pavarotti being fat is irrelevant.** How he looks has nothing to do with his singing. He could be built like a Men's Health cover model or look like an alien from another galaxy, as long as his voice has the magic, I'll listen to it.
- **Most classical operas aren't written in English.** So? Get over yourself you self-absorbed Anglo-centric cultural barbarian (Sorry, just wanted to say that out loud. Moving on...) Many of the classical composers were Italian or French. Ergo, they didn't write in English. What's the big deal? Look up the words, read a translation and enjoy the music. It's no big deal.
- **You might also notice that it isn't all that common to see opera singers using a microphone.** They have to project their voice across the whole opera house so whispering isn't really an option for them... Besides, in stark contrast to most pop singers, they actually stay on key when they turn up the volume.
- **Opera works are stories, stories that encompass human emotions and situations.** Some are serious and heart-tearing, others light and humorous. I like stories. I like them in books and

movies but also in opera. Not so much stage plays though. For some reason, I never really enjoyed those.

- **"Nessun Dorma" is IMHO the best part of Puccini's "Turandot",** which is a piece about a wickedly cruel woman (haven't we all known or loved one?) and a prince falling in love with her. You can translate it with "None shall sleep" which rings in my ears as a powerful yet elegant sentence. Did I also mention I love good writing?

What on earth does this have to do with martial arts?

Glad you asked: *it's all about skill and talent meeting training.*

You don't become such an amazing opera singer without years of hard, hard training. Obviously you need talent and Pavarotti had that in spades, but that just doesn't cut it. You need to work your butt off for **years** to pull off what he did. And then make it your own; breathe life into it instead of simply imitating those who came before you.

Years of dedicated, hard work + talent = world class skill. That's something I admire in all art forms, martial or otherwise. Here's why:

I consider myself moderately talented. When I started training, I was stiff, slow, uncoordinated and had poor balance. I was strong for my age but that was about it. No other redeeming qualities besides being too stubborn to give up.

I wasn't the best fighter out there when I competed. Loads of people were better than me. I'm also not the best player in the arts I practice; my teachers outclass me with one hand tied behind their backs. Nor am I the best writer or teacher in the world. That's just not me and I know it.

I'm also perfectly OK with this. You have to know your strengths and weaknesses and not try to be somebody you're not. There's also no shame in coming out and saying *"I can't teach you this, go to that guy because he's way better than me."* It doesn't mean I suck blocky nuts at that part of the curriculum. It only means somebody else is better. What's wrong with saying that? I think it's perfectly reasonable to expect there's somebody out there who makes you look like a beginner at what you do best. There are a couple billion people on the planet after all. What makes you so special, little snowflake?

Even though I'm not the most gifted guy around, I worked really hard for any skill I have now. It didn't come naturally; I earned it with blood sweat and tears. I was also too stubborn to quit. I figured I would eventually get to a point where I actually have something worthwhile to share.

All this to say that I know what it means to train hard in the martial arts. When I see other people training just as hard or harder still, it's something I admire even if it's in another art form.

In the presence of greatness

In the movie "Good Will Hunting" Stellan Skarsgård plays a gifted math professor who discovers a working-class, delinquent math genius played by Matt Damon. In one scene, he curses the day they met, forcing him to realize he's as an ant to a man by comparison.

I'm not like that. I actually enjoy watching people who are so much better than me. I see it as something to strive for, even though I might never reach that level. And in the mean time, I can enjoy watching something amazing. Because that's what it is when you see somebody truly gifted who also worked his ass off to take his talent all the way. That's when you're in the presence of greatness, witnessing something unique. Instead of being envious, I feel it's a reason to celebrate the human potential.

These are some of the people I feel are at that level:

- Rob Kaman is the one who really got me interested in muay Thai and I still consider him one of the greatest ever. He fought pretty much everybody and rarely lost. Though he's best known for his leg kick, there's another thing I admire even more in him as a fighter: his amazing sense of timing. He didn't do spectacular stuff, he mostly stuck to basic techniques but always seemed to time them just right. Awesome.

- Pak Tristan is one hell of a guy. His level of mastery of several arts is extremely rare. I know, most of you never heard of him. He's not on the seminar circuit and doesn't appear in the magazines. But his martial arts skills are some of the best I've ever seen. Look up this post on my blog and watch a video that shows him doing a kata several decades ago. The way he does the form is enough to give you pause but there's more: In his first movement, the pin on his gi falls off, right in front of his feet (you see him picking it up in the end). He does the entire form around it, perfectly…

- Erik Paulson is simply on another level as a teacher. He's a living encyclopedia of martial knowledge, techniques and training drills. But he also keeps on tweaking and adapting his material instead of rehashing the same stuff. As far as teachers are concerned, he's way up there.

When you look around, you'll be amazed at what some unique individuals are capable off: painters, sculptors, athletes but also martial artists and fighters. I'm inspired when I see such people weaving their magic. It makes me want to train more and get better at what I do.

UPDATE: I didn't find the video right away but here's one that definitely needs to be on this list. Risuke Otake, Shihan of Katori Shinto Ryu.

Look for the clip on YouTube where you can see him practice against the naginata. His movement is just off the scales: the precision and footwork is mind-blowing. It just doesn't get any better than this.

I first saw him several decades ago in the BBC documentary "Way of the warrior". He left an incredible impression on me then and time hasn't changed my opinion one bit. It only strengthened it.

The art in martial arts, Part Two

Garry commented this on my "The Art in Martial Arts" post:

While I agree that its impressive when you meet or train with a naturally talented athlete and almost impossible to compete with them on a level playing field, personally, I'm no longer as sure about the "art" element in martial arts. I think that the influence of scientific method on the study and practice of martial arts has become the standard starting point for students on their journey of discovery and I'm not sure whether this will prove to be positive or negative in their evolution. Many principles of movement are common across styles even if their emphasis and application varies. The moral and ethical principles prevalent in a society will always inform the way people learn and practice and create. Today, knowledge is everywhere on the Internet and people don't have to undertake epic journeys to find competent martial practitioners. As to how many of these powerful warriors are "artists" I am not sure. Perhaps Oscar Wilde's comments best elucidate my point, "All art is completely useless". By their very nature, martial arts are practical methods for self defense and therefore, are not art in the Wildean sense. I think martial methods or practices are a better generic term. But then again, what do I know; relatively speaking I'm fairly useless myself.

I think it depends on your definition of art. I touched upon it in the first part of my post already; for me it's about skill and talent coming together. It's what differentiates the commoners like us from the artists I listed. It's one of the ways to define "art" and has been valid throughout the ages. From Wikipedia's definition:

Traditionally skill of execution was viewed as a quality inseparable from art and thus necessary for its success; for Leonardo da Vinci, art, neither more nor less than his other endeavors, was a manifestation of skill.

That's what I'm talking about: skill of execution is just as important as the end result.

My whole point was that most of us don't get to that stage, where we can perform our martial art at such a level that it becomes art. Much in the same way as Baryshnikov or Nureyev could take pretty much any ballet performance to a higher level.

Bringing it back to the topic: I'm just as impressed by Kaman's sense of timing in the ring as Risuke Otake's mastery of the blade. *What* they do isn't as important as *how* they do it. To get to that level of skill, you need not only talent but also enormous amounts of training.

Another example is my tai chi chuan teacher. He kicks my ass in class, goes home to grab a steel needle and then "scratches a bit" on huge zinc plates to create wall-filling works of art for which he has received high praise. Whether this is the kind of art you like or not is irrelevant; it takes enormous amounts of technical skill to do.

The scientific method used in martial arts training and the availability of knowledge is another issue for me, one that isn't immediately relevant to this topic. The way I see it, you can give somebody all the information he needs to become a world class martial artist, it doesn't mean he'll get there. He'll still need a certain amount of talent and decades of hard work.

Hell, in every class I tell my students exactly what they need to do to avoid certain mistakes. But that doesn't mean they do something with that information. Or if they manage to do one specific part correctly, they mess up another. Again, those decades of training are what it takes to achieve mastery. On top of that, there isn't just one correct way of doing things. In most cases, you have numerous options. So your personal interpretation and expression of the material is one additional factor in turning it into art.

Though I agree that for many people it's just self defense or sports, in my mind that doesn't mean it can't also be an art form.

Training bloopers

Sometimes when you're training, the Force is with you that day: everything you do is right, your training partner can't land a shot on you and you're the reincarnation of Bruce Lee, Musashi and Bodidharma all in one.

Usually, just around the time you think nothing can go wrong, something does. If you're lucky, only your ego gets a dent. If you're not, it's injury time.Sometimes, it's your own damn fault that things go south but not always; bad things sometimes happen for no reason.

Here are two examples of mine.

- I was sparring with one of my students who was in preparation for a competition. We were working on getting him used to fighting an aggressive, hard-working yet elusive opponent. So I was moving in and out constantly, throwing both long and short combinations, changing angles and targets all the time, etc. I was feeling pretty good about myself because I managed to block almost everything my student dished out and landed a lot of my techniques. Next thing I know, he blocks my leg kick perfectly on his raised knee and a searing pain makes me feel like I broke my shin bone in half. I look down to check it isn't dangling there in two pieces but it turns out I'm lucky after all; my shin is intact though it hurts like hell. I suck it up and keep going but I couldn't kick anymore with that leg for two weeks.
- I train at home every day and have a set of warm up routines I do. I often change bits of them to experiment with new ideas, but the core is the same. I've been doing them for over 20 years now. One day, I go through them like usual. I don't mean going through the motions, I'm doing things right and my body is warming up well. After I'm done, I sit down on a small chair to put on my other training shoes (lighter ones so I don't mess up the heavy bag) and blow out my back. I didn't drop down on the chair, I wasn't

131

carrying anything heavy, nor did I twist my spine. I just sat down as I always do and felt my back give out on me. It took months and months of work to get it fixed.

These kinds of "Oops..." moments happen to everybody. Usually, as you get more experienced, they happen a bit less often. But you should always expect them to sneak up on you when you least expect it.
As with my two examples, the results can be painful and take a long time to heal. Though that's not always the case; sometimes you only take a blow to your ego. For example:

A long time ago, I used to line up my students near the end of class and have them perform techniques, answer questions, and so on. The format was more or less like a pop quiz in school. One of those times, I asked a student to perform a spinning back kick he had been working on. Despite my verbal pointers, he kept making the same mistake so I told him to sit back down and watch me demonstrate the right way.

I got into my fighting stance and focused on the technique.

I twisted my feet to start the spinning movement.

I turned my hips and rotated my spine next.

Just as I whipped my leg around, I leaned too far back with my upper body and my momentum swept me off my feet. I landed on my butt with a resounding thud.

As I got up, I heard the giggles and suppressed laughter from my students. I laughed it off, did the technique again and we bowed out.

My ego didn't enjoy the feeling of humiliation after messing up the kick in front of all my students. But I figured it was my own fault so I decided to stop being a baby and focus on fixing the problem: I practiced the kick intensively for months on end and haven't lost my balance using it ever since.

Martial arts in every day life

On an email list I'm on, we were discussing the long term changes and evolution you go through in the body mechanics you learn in your art. A lot of ideas were tossed around and here's something I ended up writing:

My teacher once told me we're all doing nothing but a Western interpretation of how you should train Chinese arts. When he lived in Hong Kong, he'd spend all his time with his teacher. They'd train for hours on end, he'd go into the hills with him and train there, talk history, techniques and strategy, etc. If you have such a training regimen and can keep it up your entire life, it's a far cry from us, Western schmucks, who can only manage a few hours a day at best. So I don't think it's realistic to want to move like the Chinese teachers who've been training 4, 5, 6 hours a day for decades on end. You gotta pay your dues first.

I sincerely believe this is true. There are no shortcuts if you want to be as good as some of the most impressive martial artists out there. For the most of us, that's just not in the cards: we have to work, have families and friends, etc. Being a full time martial artist is not really a common career here in the West.

Somebody replied that you should apply your martial arts training in every day life, seek out every opportunity to practice: As you reach for a glass of water, work on your structure, your breathing, etc. I understand the concept well enough and to a large degree do this myself. But I feel there is a lot of misunderstanding about the very idea of applying martial arts in daily life. Here's what I replied:

This is one of the things I only agree with up to a certain point. I believe this type of training has a lot of value. Hell, I flipped the light switch on and off with my feet for a long time when I was younger, much to the annoyance of my family. But it sure did benefit my kicking techniques.

However, I think there's a limit to how far you can take this before you hit the law of diminishing returns. At that point, your time is better spent actually training in the style you're learning. E.G.: If I spend fifteen minutes getting every movement right as I walk to the kitchen and drink a glass of water, I won't get anything done. This means everything takes more time, which means I have less time to actually train in my art.

In contrast, if you spend an extra fifteen minutes training your art, do it right and have a good teacher (and some more qualifiers), after a while you won't be able to pick up that glass of water in the wrong way.

I'm simplifying, I know, but only to make a point: Martial arts systems didn't come into existence to find a more efficient way to do every day things like picking up a glass to drink water from it. I know this is the theory that is gaining ground the last few years but I don't buy it. I firmly believe martial arts have fighting/combat/self-defense as the main goal and focus.

There is obviously overlap into daily/other activities but then again, these can be arts in and of themselves, not necessarily compatible ones: I have nothing of respect for somebody who masters origami or ikebana. But I really doubt they use the exact same body mechanics as a karate sensei. Mental focus, sure. But the overlap is perhaps not as big as some might think.

Obviously, you are free to disagree with me but instead of getting better at picking up glasses, I'd rather go to my garage or to class and train a bit more. I think it's more productive.

Martial arts in every day life, Part Two

After my first post on martial arts in every day life, I received a fair bit of comments. Dennis, a tai chi brother of mine, left me a lot of ideas to think about. Here are his comments and my replies:

Would the most impressive martial artists out there and/or full time marital artists turn their martial arts "training" on and off depending on whether they were suited up at in the gym: maybe not. Would some aspects, awareness for example, be "on" at almost all times? Maybe. If it's body mechanics we're talking about would they really bend, lift, move differently because they were not "in training". That might depend on how you think about it (I'll get to that in a minute).

The aspects you mention would certainly be "on" most of the time, regardless of where that martial artist would be. At least, that would be the goal. If not, what's the point in training?

As for the body mechanics, there certainly is a lot of overlap between training and daily life. However, when was the last time you did anything resembling our version of "snake creep down" in your daily life? I'm exaggerating but my point is that the overlap is not 100%.

Maybe the point where you would disagree depends on some assumptions that are at least relative: first who says you have to "seek out" the opportunity to practice – again with regard to body mechanics, doesn't training become unconscious and automatic in terms of how you move transfer force, use leverage, etc.?

It sure does. A personal example: I use "seven stars" footwork all the time in daily life. It's almost second nature now. But you'll almost never catch me using it *exactly* like we practice it in class. I'd look like a fool, zigzagging all over the place like that.

Some parts indeed become automatic but (for me at least) they are never as good as when I'm actually training or using them in the martial context they were created for. But I think that's only to be expected.

Your argument against the time efficiency pre-supposes that it's faster for example to turn on/off the light with a hand: maybe. Maybe it wouldn't matter much. My point above is that walking to the kitchen to drink a glass of water wouldn't necessarily involve additional time. (And I thought that I was only one turning light switches on/off with my feet.)

It wouldn't necessarily take up more time but in all probability, it will:

- If I do it practicing my tai chi, I have to move slowly. So, it takes more time.
- If I want to practice other arts, I'll probably go faster. But unless I get it right the first time, I'll start over until I do whatever I'm practicing correctly. Personally, I'm rarely, if ever, happy with my first attempt. So once again, I lose time.

It's subjective (maybe fanciful:-), I know, and based as much on my own imagination as anything else, but – at least in the case of Tai Chi – it could be that as an integrative art (martial as well as therapeutic and philosophical) it was a matter of typical Asian elegance and efficiency that the hardness of Kung Fu could be blended with the softness of Taoist Yin-Yang theory and the practice of the two offering the therapeutic benefits of Chi Gung at the very same time. It could be a myth that the martial arts of old had nothing but free time to train; most perhaps also had families to tent to, "jobs" and other demands – horses to tend, wood to chop, water to carry. If they be warriors of some sort, wouldn't it be handy to have a type of training that served the dual purposes of rehabilitation (I am assuming there were lots of injuries in that line of work) as well as martial abilities. If they be priests, wouldn't it be handy to have a type of meditative, contemplative, healing practice that also happened to offer transferable self-defense skills. Would it be any different for the regular Joe who had to chop wood and carry water or at least work in the field or the woods for sustenance?

I understand the rationale behind this theory but I think the martial side came first and the things you mention are derivatives, fortunate byproducts. As in:

- Consistently train hard and you'll get in good enough shape to defend yourself.
- Because you get in shape, you are healthier and have fewer injuries.
- If you do have injuries, you quickly notice that adapted training often improves your condition. And the therapeutic aspect is born…
- Because you train hard (and beat a few guys in a couple fights), you become more confident and at peace.
- If you have to go into combat, the PTSD and other psychological damage can drive you towards religion or meditative practices. And yet another aspect is added to the art…

I know I'm oversimplifying but only do so to make my point. It's probably not as black and white as I make it out to be. Also, we'll never know as nobody alive today was there when tai chi was "created". So all we can do is post our theories.

That said, I'm a firm believer in Bob Orlando's cycle of fighting techniques => fighting system=> martial art=> martial sport and then the cycle starts over. So that probably colors my opinion on this subject a bit.

It also seems to me that the accomplished Tai Chi guys of old would have been aware that the hard style training systems too often tend to create the opposite of what they intend: rather than fit warriors they often produce injured victims.

The longer I train, the less I see the border line between hard and soft styles. So I don't really know if this statement is valid or not. I don't think it is, but I could be wrong.

And lastly, then or now, what's the most likely need for the average guy doing the work on a day to day, minute by minute basis? To be able to relax, be present and adapt, or to be able to deliver the decisive blow? It's possible that martial arts training is as much about dealing with the forces encountered in daily life as it is dealing with a jab-cross-hook combination (or in the case of our current fascination with grappling, a favorite take-down move). Thanks for the topic, great thought generator!

I agree with you on what the average guy needs. But I don't think tai chi would be his first choice for that. It's way too demanding for that. There are so many other ways to achieve relaxation or presence of mind, all of them more accessible than tai chi.

My overall view is this:

There is clearly overlap between martial arts training and daily life and that's good. But I don't think it's black and white. Trying to apply your martial arts skills to *everything* you do in daily life in the hope of getting better at the arts *doesn't make sense to me*. It violates the specificity principle, which I firmly believe in. You get better at martial arts by training martial arts, **not** by swimming or cycling. And certainly not by picking up a glass of water in the kitchen.

Does that mean you shouldn't try to pick up that glass in conformity to what you learn in your art? Not at all. It means that you shouldn't spend 15 minutes on it. Because if you have 15 minutes to spare, drinking the glass takes 1 minute, leaving you with 14 minutes to actually train martial arts.

Which one do you think is more effective?

Comments policy: Meet the Lord of the Land

Since my post on Penn & Teller's PENN & TELLER: BULLSHIT! "Martial Arts" TV show, there has been an increase of comments on my blog. Most were about that post, some were about older ones. That's all good, I appreciate the feedback. It's one of the coolest things about blogging: people from all over the world interact with you.

Some of you just drop a line; others give a detailed explanation of what they're thinking. Regardless, I enjoy talking to you about the things I'm passionate about or interested in. So let's make it perfectly clear: *Feel free to comment as much as you like!* However, there are a few things you have to understand:

- **Every comment is read and approved by me.** It's more time consuming than automatically approving comments but it helps keep spam down and it allows me to talk to you. Which is the whole point of allowing comments to begin with, so I plan on keeping things like this.
- **I get plenty of email.** Answering mail takes up time. My time is limited and I don't want to waste any more if it than I absolutely have to.

Why do I mention this?

Because the Penn & Teller post generated a ton of reactions, but only a fraction were approved. Why? There are many reasons, here's a short list:

- **They were spam.** 'Nough said.
- **They were useless.** I don't need to know you just did number one on the toilet. Nor do my readers need to know that.
- **They were a recap of everything I wrote.** Ehm… I know what I wrote, no need to repeat it.
- **They were uncool.** Mr. Yetman's comment comes to mind.

139

That's the first and last time I'm allowing such a comment. See next bullet.

- **They were going to incite a flame war.** A truckload of comments went back to Mr. Yetman. Some were very polite and well reasoned. Others were very crude and inflammatory. I understand all those reactions but I chose to end the thread and didn't publish any one of them. Why? Because all that needed to be said was in the reply I wrote. He's letting it rest and as a result, so am I. Anything that gets added to that comment thread will only rekindle the flames. Nobody, I repeat, nobody benefits from that. So the thread ends. Period.

- **They were disrespectful.** If you can't argue without becoming snarky or insulting, please find another blog to do so. Don't get me wrong, I *love* sarcasm and all kinds of dark humor. But I *loathe* ad hominem attacks. You can do the one, but not the other here.

There were over 50 such comments. In other words, I had to invest a lot of time in moderating everything. As of right now, I'm not going to do that again. So let's start off anew...

Meet the Lord of the Land, aka Me.

Hi, my name is Wim Demeere and I'm the Lord of the Land on my blog. If you like, think of me as sitting on a throne, looking at you with a dark gleam in my eye. I'm sitting on that throne because it's rightfully mine: *I own this blog.*

I pay for the domain name and hosting, I write the content, I'm the guy who fixes things when they get broken, etc. I'm the boss, I'm in charge, I'm the man. So far, so good, right? But, enlightened despot that I am, you are more than welcome in these lands of mine.

In fact, you're getting everything here for free: the content, my time, my responses to your comments, it's all here for free. Isn't that just flat out awesome? I mean, it's not like I don't have anything else to do: I'm a self-employed personal trainer. That means that every minute I don't spend working, I don't make a single buck. Nada, nothing, zip. Now I don't really mind that because I thoroughly enjoy blogging and talking to you. But there are limits to my benevolence and we just reached them.

As of right now, I'm putting on my despot hat a bit more firmly and will leave the enlightened part to more intelligent people. I'll explain in a bit but the gist of it is this:

I am the Lord of the Land and my will is law.

If you like, picture me waving a big-ass broadsword over my head, wearing lots of leather and fur. I'm also sporting about 50 pounds of additional rock-hard, body-building muscle and my voice thunders in an Austrian accent as I declare this. The funky, horned helmet, and silly look on my face is optional; it's your imagination so knock yourself out...

Anyway, what does this all mean? In reality, not much will change. I'll still blog about the same things and you're still more than welcome to participate in the comments section. But I'll also implement some basic rules:

- **I'm Lord of the Land and my will is law.** I just wanted to say that again because it sounds cool, yeah! But I mean it. Anything I say is how it will be, like it or not. And like all despots and tyrants, I reserve the right to break or ignore my own rules. Because, say it with me, **I'm Lord of the Land and my will is law!** *The crowd roars!!!*
- **This is not a forum.** You don't come here and spout your bile or trash people's names as is common practice on all the forums. I'll banish you from here in a heartbeat.
- **This is not a democracy.** You don't get a vote unless I give you one (which I often do in polls.) Don't come whining to me when I don't publish a comment of yours or something "isn't fair". Because I'll get all Carlos Mencia on you and kick you to the back of the line. (50 points for those who get this one...)
- **Freedom of speech is what I allow you to say.** Meet the little dictator in me. Freedom of speech is dear to my heart but I've

seen it raped and abused too often on the Internet. You can say whatever you want, but I have the overruling power to refuse to publish your comment. If I don't like it, I most certainly will. So think twice before you submit your comment...

- **Show some goddamn respect.** I hate bullies, loudmouths, arrogant pricks, trolls and their ilk. If you act like one, I'll drive you from my lands shouting "You. Shallnot. PASS!!!" all the way. This is **my** land, **my** house. *You're a guest* and I'll be as good a host as I can. But you have to behave and show some respect to me and more importantly, all the other guests.

- **Don't go away mad, just go.** If you don't like it, find another place to comment. The Internet is huge! There are plenty of blogs, sites and forums where you can express yourself in the way you prefer. I try to avoid going where I'm not wanted and advise you to do the same. No hard feelings, really. But life's too short for infantile bickering and screaming arguments in a comments section of some blog. Discussing and talking things through, yes. But not juvenile "You suck!" yelling contests. If you can't handle this, just go elsewhere.

As Austin Powers would say "I'm spent!" I'll not come back on this topic again, I think I made my point...

NOTE:

I hesitated adding this post to the book but eventually included it. What decided it for me was sitting at the breakfast table with Barry Eisler and talking about how humor can fix problems you sometimes have a hard time solving in any other way, especially on the internet. He mentioned a couple examples of replies he'd written to people on his blog and Facebook page, where it would have been easy to get angry but he still took the high road. More often than not, this is more effective at handling vicious, hurtful feedback than anything else you can think of.

I agreed and showed him this post. He laughed all the time while reading it (especially when he saw the Schwarzenegger picture from

"Conan The Barbarian".) and told me it was good writing. So I decided to add it to this volume.

The other reason is this: while reading this book, you might feel very strongly about some of my opinions and decide to tell me about it. If you haven't visited my blog before, you won't have a baseline to compare my comments policy to. With this piece here, you know what to expect.

Make no mistake, you're more than welcome to drop a line on my blog. But read this comments policy again first. It's better for all of us that way. Thanks.

Martial arts reality check

This post needs some background before I come to the martial arts stuff, so bear with me...

This weekend, I attended my brother-in-law's wedding. He married a beautiful bride and they had a great day. The wedding party went on until early morning and everybody had a great time. Especially me, because:

- I got to do my imitation of the Will & Carlton dance with everybody watching. The roar of laughter that followed must mean my performance was good enough. (I choose not to consider any other possibilities, thank you very much...)
- I didn't have to drive so I could drink a bit more than usual.
- As a result, I danced even sillier than usual. Which resulted in people laughing very, very hard. Which only egged me on to bust some more dance moves. And so on.
- I inhaled helium and spoke in a funny voice, along with a few other people. They were a lot funnier than me but we still laughed so hard somebody actually fell from a chair.
- I got to slow-dance with my beautiful lady on a huge dance floor. Lots more fun than dancing in the kitchen or living room like we usually do.
- I was with people who are close to me for the entire day and we all had a great time together.

In short, I had a blast. In fact, it had been a long time since I was able to kick back and relax like that. After so many years of working on awareness and prevention, I don't feel at ease anymore in a crowd. Simply because there's such a high potential for violence when lots of people get together, particularly when there's a lot of alcohol involved, which was most certainly the case here. It usually goes something like:

- One drunk spills his beer over another and the fight is on.
- Somebody eyes another guy's woman (or the guy thinks she's being eyeballed) and fists start flying.
- You're having way too much fun for some people so they decide to fuck up your day by picking a fight.

And I'm not even mentioning pickpockets, gangs or other criminals. Go to any big public gathering and they're bound to be there too.

But at this wedding, it was invitation only and there were no assholes among the guests. Even the wildest drunk didn't come close to needing to be calmed down. And party-crashers couldn't sneak up on us; I'd have spotted them long before they even came close to me. So I got to relax, let down my guard and just had a blazing good time. A rare occasion for me.

For the record, when we left and went to the parking lot, I cranked up the awareness and prepared for trouble. I know when it's time to have fun but also when that time has passed...

What's the point, dude?

The point is: *every now and then, you need to do a reality check.*

In my opinion and also my experience, people in the martial arts and self defense community are very bad at this. In fact, I'll raise my hand right now and confess to be a big sinner in this regard. I'm so involved and fascinated by everything concerningmartial arts, self defense and training for these two that I sometimes lose perspective.

The correct perspective is that, as far as I know, *nobody is actively trying to kill me.* This means I'm not in danger of a violent death while I'm typing this blog post. Following this logic, the only danger for violence is random violence. Random violence means:

- **I go to a store and it gets robbed.** This can happen to anybody, it's just your bad luck that you're in the wrong place at the wrong time. Shit happens.

- **I walk around in public and a street thug or criminal picks me as his victim.** Again, it can happen to anybody.
- **I get involved in social violence.** This means drunks accosting me, young bucks trying to prove themselves by mouthing off to me, etc. Again, this can happen to everybody.
- **Mr. Murphy takes me down.** I'm not going to worry about buildings crushing me during an earthquake or terrorists blowing up my apartment. There are limits to how far I'll take my awareness where I live; Belgium is not Afghanistan, though its politicians could probably be swapped with ease and without an observable difference.

There are loads more scenarios but you get the drift.

Here's the thing, for each of the first three bullets, there is a lot I can do to prevent that violent death from happening to me. In order:

- **My awareness goes up when I go to a store.** A while ago, the supermarket five minutes from my place, the one I sometimes shop at, got robbed by three guys wielding Uzi's. Stores get robbed, period. But you have to shop somewhere. So during my shopping, I pay attention and the moment I spot firearms, I'll hit the deck and try to crawl to the back. Failing that, I'll obey the commands from the robbers. Why? Because I live in a country where I'm not allowed to carry weapons and I don't have a big "S" on my chest. Until I do, I'm not going up against three guys with machine guns. I don' think how hard my leg kick is makes any difference in such a situation. Or any other unarmed technique for that matter…
- **Public places = awareness up, radar constantly pinging.** A vast majority of violence can be avoided by spotting trouble before it can escalate. This takes knowledge and training but it can most certainly be done.
- **It's not worth it to me.** Social violence is just not worth my time, energy or the potential consequences. Sure, there are certain buttons you can push on me and it'll piss me off. I'm just like everybody else. But I'll do my damn best to walk away first. So call me a motherfucking asshole if it makes you feel better. I'll just go

home and laugh while I walk away towards something you're missing: a life worth living.

The common thread in all of the above solutions is that it takes work on your part. Prevention, awareness, walking away, these are all acquired skills. They don't come naturally, unless you grew up or live in a violent society, a place where violence is an every day occurrence. In such an environment, you learn these skills real fast or you don't make it out alive. But for the most of us, that's not the case.

So we practice and practice until these skills become second nature and they're "On" all the time. Train for a bit longer still and you don't know how to turn them "Off" anymore…

Armageddon isn't here just yet.

Which brings me back to my original point: *take a reality check every now and then.* Like me at the party, you too can relax from time to time. Chances are that as you're reading this post:

- Nobody is trying to kill you either.
- You're not being molested in some dark alley.
- There isn't a horde of ninjas jumping out of the shadows to slice you to pieces.

All of this could happen later, when you step away from reading these words and step outside into the world again. But right now, you're probably fine. And there are other moments and places when/where you're fine too. But if you get too wrapped up in a self-defense or martial arts mindset, you no longer recognize them when they present themselves. Then they pass you by, which is a crying shame.

If enough of these pass you by, the only thing you'll do in your life is work and be on the lookout for potential violence. Okay, that's stretching things a bit but you get what I mean:

Life is to be lived.

Self defense, martial arts, *they're supposed to help you **live** your life, **not** replace it.*

My reality check reminded me of that once again. So while I'll still try to prevent and avoid violence as much as I can, I renewed my goal of living a full and rewarding life. Accordingly, I've planned my next care-free, funfunfun,I-m-gonna-have-a-blast, moments already.

How about you?

Martial arts reality check, Part Two

I ran across this piece of news.

"Police claim that when Mr Alvarez saw the police, he turned his gun on them. Over 50 shots were fired in the exchange, with 46 of them being from the policeman's guns. At least 21 of these bullets penetrated Mr Alvarez's body, wounding him in his arms, legs, abdomen and jaw. Mr Alvarez is currently in hospital, and as of last night was in a critical condition. Doctors say all the bullets miss his vital organs.

One policeman was hurt in the affray, with a bullet hitting him in the chest, and another suffered a graze on his hand from a stray bullet."

Long story short, a guy gets shot **21 times** and still survives… Just stop and imagine that for a second: *21 bullets enter your body and you don't die.* Talk about being lucky!

Granted, no vital organs were hit but the guy got shot in the arms, legs, abdomen and jaw. Even though these aren't vital organs, there are still plenty of arteries there. Even without organ damage, he could have bled out and died anyway. But he didn't.

So what?

Well, this just goes to show that you can't always predict what's going to happen when you use force, deadly or otherwise. Because let's be honest: if somebody says a couple cops are going to fire 46 shots at you, hitting you with 21, would you really think you'd survive? Nope. And in most cases you'd be right. But as this story proves, there are exceptions.

To be clear: I'm not saying you should go out and make a LEO draw on you because you just might get lucky and survive. What I'm saying is: you never know what's going to happen when the feces hits the rotating blades.

Now you might be thinking "Duh!" and that's your prerogative but my point is this: even if you accept that the most unlikely things can and will happen in a fight, **that won't stop you from making assumptions about fighting and combat.** Making assumptions is human nature and we all fall prey to this bad habit. To make matter worse, we usually *don't realize* we make these assumptions. But we sure do train according to them. And there's the problem.

I train in both combat sports and traditional martial arts because I believe they both have value. In fact, they complement each other very well, providing you distinguish between the different environments they operate in. To do that, you make up a mental image of what each of these two types of disciplines look like. You make this image by drawing from your own experience, reading, watching videos of actual fights, talking to others who share their experience, etc. All these things combine into some big-ass assumptions about what a fight looks like in a MMA match and how things are on the street in self defense situations.

Chances are good you're right on the money for some and totally wrong for others (Unless, of course, you are so totally awesome you're never, ever, EVER, wrong about anything...) But you won't know which is which until you start fighting for real, regardless of the environment and context.

Get to the point already! Shees...

Here's the rub: whatever mental map you made of the huge territory that is fighting, it's never as accurate as you think. That's OK, it's just how things work. But that doesn't mean you have to ignore this fact and move on. It's more efficient to work from the basis that your map has some **pertinently wrong** information. And you won't know it's wrong *until* you are on the spot that part of the map is pointing to. By that time, it may be too late to do anything about it though. Because the erroneous assumptions you based your training on didn't prepare you for the "Holy Crap WTH is this?!!!!" situation you suddenly encounter.

Whuh? I don't get it?

Here's an example. An exaggerated one, but bear with me.

If you base your entire self defense training on shooting your attacker, you would need a reload to put down the guy from the story. While you're busy reloading, he could still be coming at you. I doubt he'd give you the time to finish that reload… If he has a knife, things get even more interesting…

Now had you asked your firearms instructor "How many bullets does it take to stop an attacker? Would 21 be enough?", chances are he'd say "Probably,yes". Some of the firearms trainers I've seen would say "Of course! It wouldn't even take more than three bullets from a BlingBlangKapow pistol if you use the special UltraMegaKillKill load because it has mad stopping power! Yipikayee MoFo!!!"

But we now know this isn't always true…

Granted, I'm exaggerating and yes, you can pick this example apart. That's not the issue. *The issue is that you would likely never have thought it would have taken 21 bullets to stop a guy.* You would have assumed less then 21 was more than enough to finish the job. Which brings forth the big question:

If you are wrong about this assumption, what else are you wrong about?

And even more importantly:

How does this affect your training and what are you doing to correct these flaws?

By the way, if you think this is a unique case, talk to Loren about the time a criminal ran a block before succumbing to a bullet through the heart. Imagine what damage he could have done had he turned to fight the cops instead of running...

Wrapping things up.

In the first part or Martial Arts Reality Check I talked about not assuming there's a ninja hiding in every shadow and actually living your life instead. It takes the occasional reality check to do that.

In this part, I'd like to suggest you're going to be flat out wrong about some of the assumptions you make about fighting and self defense. I know I've been wrong many times, chances are so have you. Even worse, just because we discovered some faulty assumptions in the past doesn't mean there aren't any left now. Remember, you won't know you're wrong unless somebody points it out to you or you encounter the problem in real life.

So every now and then, it's probably a good idea to do a reality check, to investigate if your martial arts training isn't based on assumptions that just don't cut it in real life.

The limits of martial arts knowledge and skill

When I started training, I was in awe by what I thought was going to be in store for me: I was going to learn to kick ass like Bruce Lee and Chuck Norris! Woohoo!

Things obviously didn't turn out that way and I soon discovered there was no shortcut or a guaranteed way to acquiring skill and knowledge in the martial arts.

Fast forward 25 years, the last 20 of which at a regimen of 1-5 training hours a day.

I still can't kick ass like Mr. Norris (nobody can) and I'll always be too heavy to move like Mr. Lee (No cheap shots, thanks.) As false humility is just as bad as being an arrogant prick, here goes: I think I know a little bit about the arts I train in. More than most, because of the amount of training and time spent in these arts. Less than others, meaning my seniors, my teachers, etc. The longer I train, the less people will fall in the latter category. At least, that's how it **should** be if I keep on training and progressing. It's my plan to do just that so I'm hopeful…

But what does that mean? How do you quantify it?

I don't think you can. Knowledge and skill are too difficult to pin down. Especially because these things are never written in stone:

- Skill deteriorates if you don't keep on training.
- Knowledge becomes outdated if you don't keep up to date with the latest developments.

So when you chose to live a life in the martial arts, you're always striving to learn more, get more skilled.

My teacher said it real well: you have to be a student, in the truest sense of the word. It comes from the Latin word "studere" which means "to be eager, to pursue, to desire". That's exactly the type of mindset you need to do a lifelong study of anything:

- You're always eager to learn more, to try new things.
- You pursue your dream, your quest for skill and knowledge.
- You desire it, not just want it. There's a difference.

In these last 25 years, there were numerous times when I wanted to give up, when I grew tired of all the training. Invariably, something happened that rekindled the flame (read about the arts, saw somebody do something really neat on video, got to know an amazing teacher, etc.) and I became a student once again. I plan on remaining one until the day I die.

Awesome! I'm in!

Cool, jump on board. But here's something I didn't realize when I started.

As a 13-year old,I was too young to understand this concept. When I hit my twenties, I didn't think it mattered and figured I was bad-ass anyway. In my early thirties, I discovered this first hand by meeting and training with people I call "masters". Now, nearing my forties, I think it's absolutely crucial to understand the following:

After all the time I spent training, I think I now have my equivalent of a PhD.

This implies several things:

- I've only contributed a very, **very** small piece to the overall pool of knowledge in my area of study.
- I'll **never** be able to reproduce the same depth of knowledge in other martial arts or fields.
- There is an *insanely huge amount of knowledge and skill I don't have* **and never will.**

The old saw of "the longer I study, the more I realize I don't know much" is true. It doesn't matter how good you are or how much further you go past the boundaries of current knowledge, you're still in the same boat as everybody else.

Which is why I loathe those keyboard-warriors who can't shut up in the forums or guys with 5 years of training who insist you call them "Master". If you take one look at your own training, you can only come to a handful of conclusions:

- I've still got a long way to go…
- I may be right about what I know but that doesn't mean somebody else is wrong. He's probably pushing on a boundary in a totally different specialty than me.
- I know Jack about the hundreds of other martial arts and combat sports I **don't** practice. People who do train in them are much better placed to comment on them.
- I'll never be as good as I want to be.

Damn, you're a spoilsport!

Not really. I'm not writing this to make you feel bad. I just happen to think it's the absolute truth. And it applies to me just as well as you. So once again, we're all in the same boat.

Instead of seeing this as a negative thing, it should spur you on: Precious few people will ever get to the same exact level of knowledge you do. Regardless of how much of how far you get, making it that far is its own reward.

Special thanks to Kris Wilder for the inspiration.

Why I'm not a martial arts millionaire (yet)

In the last few weeks, a couple things came together and the result is this (long) post. Here's the list of events:

- Somebody asked about blogging and part of my response was this:

If you really want to make money blogging, you'll have to work hard and probably go for business models that aren't always cool. Not my thing, but to each his own.

- I had a discussion with another instructor/author about training methodology, cross training and the value of traditional martial arts. It took me a while before I figured out we weren't talking about the same thing. I think he's right in what he said. I also think I'm right in what I said.
- Branimir Tudjan said the following in the interview I did with him:

First I would like to thank you for your interest in my MOSS video and for conducting this interview. You know, in the so called martial arts world which is nowadays unfortunately full of big ego "grandmasters" or "guru's" and where every "expert" perceives others (and their systems) as a potential threat or less "realistic & effective" system then their own, it's a pleasure to meet a person and a colleague like yourself who is competent, mature, confident and open minded. I am also genuinely impressed with your work with Paladin Press.

- Somebody got the ball rolling on important life lessons, things that suddenly clicked. I wrote:

Mine was: just because I'm right about something, somebody else isn't necessarily wrong about the same subject. And vice versa.

All these things combined are what lead up to the title of my post here.

Why I'm not a martial arts millionaire (yet)

The short of it: I don't want it at any price. The goal doesn't justify the means.

If you want to succeed in business, you have to work real hard and be willing to make tough moral decisions. I don't mind the working hard part, that's not an issue. The moral decisions thing is another can of worms. I'm not saying you have to be an evil overlord to make a good living in this business (and yes, martial arts is also a business if you do it for a living) but it can lead you down that road to make a quick buck. Here's why:

Regardless of how good you are in your art.

Regardless of how good your books or videos are.

Regardless of how well intentioned you are.

There's an undeniable truth you'll run into again and again: **Those things are not enough to ensure financial success.**

OK, why not?

Because making a good product is only half the work. You also have to convince people to buy it, which is what marketing is all about.

I'm not a great marketer. In fact, my ex-wife constantly told me I had to be commercial-minded, promote myself more, etc. Marketing was the part of my business I hated the most and, as a result, neglected a lot. I thought that stuff was against some martial arts code of ethics, it felt like boasting or showing off.Things I despise.

Fast forward ten years and I figured out she was right. Not only that, but I was dead wrong. There is no reason to equate martial arts teaching with living in poverty or teaching for free. There's also *no reason* why I shouldn't make a lot of money teaching the arts, writing books and making videos. I'm not ripping people off, nor am I lying to them. I can look in the mirror and say "I believe in what I teach. My stuff may not be perfect, but I believe in it." My conscience is clear.

But that isn't enough. Just because you have a good product, doesn't mean you will make money off it.

Here's a sad story:

A man who was instrumental in creating the audio compact disc sold his idea for a couple thousand to Philips. When he realized his mistake, he tried to negotiate with Philips to get a piece of the pie whenever his invention was used. He failed. Philips used it to develop the compact disc and it made them billions. The man got zip, nada, nothing.

The same goes for creating martial arts books or videos and teaching these arts: Just because you're good, doesn't mean you'll make money. People won't just buy your stuff and book you for lessons. That's just not how it works. Why? Because most of them don't know about you. *The only way for them to get to know about you is by getting your name out there, which means: marketing...*

Today's martial arts industry

In today's world, this applies in spades. If you don't market yourself, people won't know about you. As a result, they won't buy your stuff and you don't make a dime. I'm exaggerating a little, but not all that much and here's why:

Even if they *have* heard about you, the other guy (the one doing all that marketing) is somebody they've heard about a whole lot more. *Guess whose products they're most likely to buy?*

What I didn't want to hear when I was younger (and what many beginning martial arts professionals refuse to acknowledge) is that good marketing works. Commercials work. Despite the fact that we're bombarded with them, they still work. ***Even if you think they don't**,* they still have their effect on you, especially in the long run.

Because of how easy it is today to make a product, put up a website and sell it, the market has become very crowded. Open up a MA magazine, browse the Internet a bit and you'll see tons of martial arts products for sale. Usually, the ones who get the most exposure are the ones that sell best. So if you want to make some money in this business, you have no other choice but to do your own marketing. The only question left is: "what kind of marketing?

We've all seen ads that promise "Beat any opponent 100% of the time!" techniques and most people I talk to about this can't believe anybody falls for them. The reality is that people do just that, every day. This kind of marketing is very effective in getting a lot of people to buy your products. They may never buy anything from you again if you're selling crap *but you'll still have their money from that first buy.*

Despite having embraced marketing more than in the past, I refuse to do stuff like that. Simply because *I believe it isn't true.* I believe the issues regarding martial arts and self defense are complex. You can't just dumb them down to whatever you like and then claim your techniques are unbeatable. Sure, it'll sell your stuff but it's flat out not true. Things are shades of grey, not black or white.

Which brings me to my blog and why I put so much time and effort in it:

- Like I said: *just because I'm right about something, somebody else isn't necessarily wrong about the same subject. And vice versa.* Just because I like to use certain techniques and they work for me, that doesn't mean other people can't do it differently. That's why I review other instructor's products. Because it allows me to learn more about other systems, learn their point of view and perhaps gain new insights into things I already learned. If it doesn't work for me, no sweat. Maybe it'll work for you; hence my review. I'm just passing on the word. Here's the thing: *acknowledging another author's products are good doesn't invalidate mine.* Just because his stuff is good, doesn't make mine bad. I have an ego like everybody else (my girlfriend says it's pretty big) but even I can admit this. Also, the reverse is true as well: just because his stuff is bad, doesn't make mine good.

- This all means that I don't feel bad anymore promoting myself and my products. They may not be the best out there, they may not work for everybody and I know that. But I also know that I did the best I could when making them. From the feedback I've gotten, a lot of people do find them useful. So why shouldn't I promote them then?
- The caveat is honesty. I don't want to sell something for what it's not. I don't believe in ultimate systems so I won't market my stuff as such. I don't believe in "perfect solutions" so I won't claim that either. All I can do is give it my best shot, tell you what the product is for and then hope you like it and find a use for it. And I'll also tell you when I don't know something or when I think somebody else has a good answer. Hence the reviews and interviews I do here.
- But a trade off is warranted here: If I'm honest and tell you to buy somebody else's stuff instead of my own, I don't earn a living. That may be honest, but it doesn't put food on the table. OK, then I'm going to put up advertising on my blog to pay for the hosting, my time, loss of income, etc. And I'll also put up those other people's products with affiliate links so I get a (really, really) small cut if you happen to buy it. It isn't much but it's more than the alternative: nothing. Again, there's no reason why I shouldn't earn a small fee when I promote other people. Nobody loses here.
- Of course, I'd still prefer you buy my stuff too. Why wouldn't I? If I didn't want to make money with it, I wouldn't sell it. And if I'm willing to sell it, my goal is obviously to make lots of money off it. But not at any cost. So I won't tell bullshit just to make that extra sale.

Conclusion

Because this is the way I see things, I'm not earning as much money as I could. I'm not a millionaire yet.

Not a big deal; most people could have more money if they just went outside and snatched a few purses away from old ladies. Most people don't do this because they don't want to be assholes. The same applies here: you can make a lot of money, fast, but not always in an honest way? A few personal examples:

- I was asked if I wanted to sell my blog for a lot of money and have somebody else keep writing it under my name. The idea was to turn it into an Internet marketing machine with me as a brand and I still got a cut of everything. I said no. It would have been flat out deceiving people
- I've been approached repeatedly to promote products and sell them at huge commissions. The products with the highest commissions were really lame. I said no. This would have been flat out lying.
- I've had the opportunity to set up my Combat Sanshou system as an insanely commercial franchise. I'm talking about a million dollar deal, really big stuff. But I would have had to do some pretty unsavory things, so I said no. The parts of the deal that were cool are things I was planning on doing anyway, so no great loss there.

Some of you might think I'm an idiot for turning these people down. I understand, that's cool. We all have to live with our decisions.

Others will think I'm a "good guy" for not doing so. I'm not, though. I didn't act out of some sort of martial ethic or moral superiority. I refused those deals because I don't believe they are good for me in the long run, they're bad business decisions. The fact that they're morally on shaky grounds and that I would have to go against things I believe to be true is just another part of that decision.

I also won't fault others who do accept these kinds of offers. I'm not in their shoes so I can't comment. They may have valid reasons for their actions, who knows? All I can say is that it doesn't work for me.

All that said, one of my goals for 2011 is to earn a better income so I can spend more time with my kids, train with my teachers and travel abroad. My books and videos, this blog and my job are what will allow me to do those things. The more of my own stuff I sell, the more I can achieve those goals. It might take me longer than others by doing it my own way, but at least I won't have to be ashamed of myself.

How to become a martial arts expert

I stumbled upon an interesting quote today, one I think has a lot of merit for martial artists and self defense enthusiasts. Actually, it's two quotes but I'll start with one:

When we look at any kind of cognitively complex field — for example, playing chess, writing fiction or being a neurosurgeon — we find that **you are unlikely to master it unless you have practiced for 10,000 hours.**

I truly believe this 10.000 hour rule applies in spades if you want to become a martial arts expert. One of the reasons Loren and I got along so well when we got to know each other was because we both like to do loads of solo training.

Many practitioners only do their reps when they go to class. Then they go home and don't practice until next class. I never understood that. As a teenager, I'd come home after class and repeat the things I'd just learned. The next day, I trained those again. Partly out of fear of forgetting them (I'm a slow learner) but mainly to just get better. Some of my classmates didn't understand this was the primary reason why I made faster progress than them: I trained more.

I often tell my beginning students to do this too: practice every day. If only for 5 minutes, but do it every day. When they take my advice, it shows: sometimes in as little as a week, they make huge progress. Five minutes a day doesn't seem like much but it adds up. For some reason, we Western folks often think we're wasting our time if we don't train for at least an hour. That's just not true. Repetition is the key. You need to get your reps in, regardless of how you do so.

Loren always emphasized this in his writing and videos: get your reps in. I think he's spot on and after all these years, I still try to sneak in as many reps as I can. My girlfriend is used to me practicing at all possible moments, regardless of where we are (though I have become more discreet over the years and don't embarrass her in public too often anymore.)

I want to become a martial arts expert!

Cool, start training more! It's that simple. But at the same time, it's a lot more complex. Here's the second quote:

Those 10,000 hours have to be invested in the right *things, and as the disjointed nature of Hamming's talk underscores, the question of* **what are the right things** *is slippery and near impossible to nail down with confidence.*

This is where the plot thickens…

10.000 hours of training is a lot. You can boil it down to about three hours a day, seven days a week, for ten years straight. That's a lot of training. Let's assume you're up for it but then you run into a problem right away:

How *precisely* do you fill those ten years of training?

- What exactly should you train?
- In what order?
- Which parts should you emphasize at which stage?
- When do you know you've been training the wrong things?
- Which training methodology should you use?
- Etc.

There are tons more questions in this list, too many to sum up here, but they bring forward the main problem the second quote illustrates: *you have no way of knowing you're going about it the right way.* There's just no way you can be 100% sure you are doing the right things in your training. Anybody who claims this is trying to sell you something.

Sure, there are general blueprints you can follow and there's a huge body of work available to draw ideas from. You also have easy access to tons of experienced teachers, people who've been there and have done that. So if there ever was a time when you could find information on how to train martial arts or self defense, today is it.

But these experts aren't you. They can't be you. So they can never make the best decision for you specifically. Nobody knows better what you need than you. Of course, this implies you're honest to yourself and aren't delusional. But I believe the reasoning is valid enough: don't count on those experts to do your thinking for you.

I still want to be a martial arts expert!

Good for you! My only advice would be to ask yourself: *do you want it bad enough?*

Because 10.000 hours of training means investing a lot of time and effort. Neither are there any guarantees you'll make the right choices as far as *what* you should be training. So it might take a whole lot longer still before you reach the point where you can consider yourself an expert.

So I repeat: *how much do you want it?*

Me? I'm well past those 10.000 hours, so I think I'm entitled to speak. Do I consider myself an expert? Nope. I'm just a guy who's been training longer than many people. I learned some things along the way (I better have…), made tons of mistakes, have some skill but I still have a long way to go when I look at my teachers and others in the same field. Some of my friends have twice the amount of training that I've done and I'm nowhere near their level. Others have only a fraction of my amount of training but tons more live experience. In certain things, this makes them more skilled than me.

Frankly, I think labels like "expert" or "master" are highly overrated these days. There are very few people I personally think deserve those titles. Invariably, all of them refuse to use them. They prefer you call them by their first name. Those are the people I look up to. Them and my teachers are the people whose opinion I care about. If they say I'm going down the wrong path, I listen up. If some anonymous Internet troll talks smack about me, I couldn't care less. Life's too short to waste my time on their crap.

The best advice I can give is what my teacher wrote in one of his books:

The word "student" comes from the Latin verb "studere" which means "to be eager" or "diligent". If you want to be an expert,you'll have to become a lifelong student. He gives a couple of guidelines for this, writing that a good student:

- Practices.
- Looks and listens.
- Thinks, then asks.
- Is neither too harsh nor too soft with his training partners.
- Constantly seeks to learn, both inside and outside class.
- Trains and competes honestly.

These guidelines are not hard to understand. But I've found them sometimes very hard to follow. It's easy to be too hard on a training partner. It's also easy to become dishonest with yourself when you train. These things don't necessarily happen out of malice, they're just part of being human. When they happen to you, correct your mistakes and move on.

All I can add is that when you try to follow these guidelines, chances are good you'll not waste too many of those 10.000 hours on the wrong things.

That's it? That's all you've got?

Just one more word of advice: Above all, *have fun training*. If it isn't fun, you won't ever make it to those 10.000 hours.

Fear, self-talk and self-defense

Loren and I were talking last week and he mentioned something that would be an interesting topic to write about here. It combines the three things I mention in the title:

- Fear
- Self-Talk
- Self-Defense

Here's the thing:

We all like to think of ourselves as bad-ass mo-fo's who chew nails and spit them out as bullets. It's a nice and comforting thought but it isn't accurate: except for rare cases, most people will feel fear when they're in a self-defense situation. That fear can manifest itself in many different ways but I'm only going to focus on one of them now: negative self-talk.

Picture this situation:

You're having drinks with a couple buddies in an up-scale bar, a place where the bad guys usually don't come. You're having fun and so is everybody else there: there's nothing going on but everybody having a good time. But you do a regular radar sweep every now and then, just in case.

During one of those sweeps, something pings on the screen: one guy gives off a negative vibe. You let your sweep pass him by and then keep an eye on him in your peripheral vision. A couple of things become apparent right away:

- He's *huge*. Taller, heavier and at first glance, a lot stronger than you.
- He's from a specific Eastern-European ethnicity. One that has a large, exceedingly violent and very tough criminal element in the

city.

- He moves like he knows how to fight. The way he stays balanced, the coordination and deliberate movements, they all let you know he's busted some skulls before.
- His expression is extremely negative. His face says he's angry as hell.

So you do a quick check of your surroundings, look for routes of escape, improvised weapons, obstacles to use against him and most importantly: how to get your friends out in one piece too. You use another sweep to mask that you're looking at him for more information-gathering and something happens: *he looks right at you, giving you the evil eye.*

That little voice inside your head suddenly pipes up and says:

"Damn, he's big. He must hit really, really hard..."

Not exactly a roaring vote of confidence from your subconscious mind...

Not to leave you hanging: I managed to avoid a confrontation with that guy, even though it took a lot of maneuvering to stay clear of him. No blood, no foul and all is well that ends well.

Negative self-talk

That's what Loren and I were discussing: sometimes, that voice in your head just starts undermining your efforts to avoid problems and defend yourself. If you listen to it, it becomes so much harder to get out of the situation in one piece.

Why does this happen? Hard to say, there could be many different reasons for it.

Think this doesn't apply to you? Think again. It can happen to anybody: people with no training or experience and experts with hundreds of violent encounters under their belt.

In the next part of this post, I'll discuss some of the ways to deal with this but for now; I'd like to ask you to share your own experiences:

What did the voice inside your head say when something like this happened to you?

Just write it down somewhere and then read part two of this post.

Fear, self-talk and self-defense, Part Two

In the first part of "Fear, self-talk and self-defense", I mentioned the negative things that can pop into your mind when you're about to go toe-to-toe with somebody. Like I explained there, it can happen to anybody. It doesn't really matter how well trained you are or how much experience you have. Sometimes, your subconscious mind just decides to mess with you. But what can you do about it? Here are some ideas.

Accept it.

Start by accepting, at a gut level, that this can happen to you. You don't have to *like* it, that's not what I mean. But you have to accept that this can happen to any of us, including you.

Usually, when I this to students or clients, I get a "Yeah, yeah, I got it." type of response. Which is fine by me; it's not my own training we're talking about. It's their ass on the line when they're about to be shredded into little pieces by some behemoth street-punk who's stoned out of his mind. Unfortunately, t that point it'll be too late to do anything about that little voice in your head as it sabotages your confidence by pointing out just how big that guy is.

The thing is, you can increase your odds of avoiding this situation. All you need to do is anticipate it happening. To do that, you have to start by truly accepting you might fall prey to this negative kind of self-talk.

Unfortunately, we all have a tendency to avoid accepting such facts. I guess it's human nature to ignore an ugly truth rather than deal with it. If you're real honest about it and can admit to this line of thinking here's a way to break that self-induced illusion of being a fearless god of war. Though I have to warn you: it won't be a fun ride.

- Close your eyes and relax.

- Focus on your body, relax your muscles and feel them. Feel the air going in and out of your lungs, feel your heart pumping blood throughout every part of you with each beat.
- Now picture everything you love in life in vivid detail: your husband/wife, your children, your family, job, hobbies, etc.
- When you have all this in your mind, say out loud:

I will die, they too will die, everything dies.

And then you imagine the great, empty void of space and time. The nothingness we all end up in, until the end of time…

If you can accept this, truly accept it for the fact of life it is (let's leave religion out of this conversation, thank you), then you're ahead of the game. It's not a fun thing to do (and you can blame Jim Butcher for giving me the inspiration in one of his books.) but it helps putting things in perspective and face reality instead of holding on to comfortable illusions.

Illusions about self defense and your own skills are no different from this. Accept that you too, not matter how tough, trained or experienced you are, can fall prey to these negative thoughts when you find yourself in a self-defense situation.

If you don't want to believe me, here are some comments from Loren on the previous post. Believe him. His credentials are as good as it gets.

When I was a cop, there were a few times when I was dealing with people who were about to go violent that I would think, "Man, I should have trained harder." In fact, I was already training as hard as I possibly could, but I was training for competition. Even as a young, fit guy in my 20s, I had had enough experience as a military policeman in Saigon, Vietnam and as a city cop in Portland, Oregon, to know that there was a big difference between sport and reality. After about four or five of these uncomfortable moments, I gave up competition and devoted my training to the street.

When I was working on my book Deadly Force Encounters, my coauthor Dr.

Artwohl and I found that 26 percent of officers involved in a deadly force incident, roughly one out of four, had thoughts that were intrusive and distracting during their shootings. Often the intrusive thoughts were bizarre, such as one officer who said that when a man shoved a gun in his face, his first thought was, "Wow, that is just like my partner's gun. I wonder where he got it."

In the heat of battle, many people think of their family. One police officer said that during a gunfight, he had a vision of his three-year-old boy toddling around in front of him in his pajamas. These intrusive thoughts are not always distracting; sometimes they can serve as an inspiration or motivation, as in the case of another police officer who was shot in the face. He said that a sudden thought about his young son motivated him to get up and return fire, killing his assailant. Psychologists don't' exactly know why we have these intrusive thoughts. We do know that positive self-talk has been proven to be highly beneficial, the most important of which is, "I will survive and keep going, no matter what." Often, wounded police officers report that this was all they heard in their minds after they were shot, and it was essential to their survival. These are the kind of intrusive thoughts that we must program into our minds if we are to survive in combat.

Train for it

Now that you've dealt with the fact that your own sub-conscious mind might get in the way when you're in a street-fight, here are some ideas you can use to prepare for it in training:

- **Positive self-talk.** Like Loren said in the above comment, try to overwrite the negative thoughts preemptively with positive self-talk. I don't mean telling yourself "I have mad skillz, I am teh Mazter!!!" but more along the lines of "I'll do whatever it takes to get home alive." or "I'm not going down, no matter what." or "I'm not going to give up, ever."
- **Educate yourself.** Read books, talk to others who've been there, watch documentaries. In short, find out how it was for those who already experienced this and learn about the solutions they found effective.
- **Don't be a slacker.** You can't fool your subconscious mind. If you haven't been training regularly, it knows you haven't. No matter how much youlie to yourself, it knows you haven't been

putting in the hours of blood, sweat and tears at the gym these last few weeks. It therefore knows that you aren't as ready for violence as you could be. That often triggers it to spout off some negative thoughts to express the doubts it has on how ready you are right this instant at handling that ugly looking mugger you just spotted eyeballing you…

- **Don't die in training.** When you do scenario training (or any other training), don't "die" when you mess up. Don't train to fail, train to overcome no matter what. Even if you get knocked down or you would have been killed in the training drill, keep on going until you "win". Obviously, you need a supervising party in those training sessions to avoid things from escalating when you and your training partner go at it.

- **When you do fight, fight for more than yourself.** Here's what Clint said about fighting five guys when he was the bouncer in a tough bar.

I started thinking about my kids and if I would see them again. A thousand things rushed through my mind. They separated and started walking towards me trying to circle up and surround me. Five guys, three my size, one older and smaller, one medium sized and young. In my head I am screaming get the fuck out of there, but I can't run, not what I was hired to do.

They got up on three sides of me and the older one asked if I knew him. I said "Nope , don't think I have ever seen you before." He then told me we went to school together and I made his life a living hell. I was at a loss. I asked him where he was from, he said Amarillo. When I told him I wasn't from there he wouldn't believe me. Man I was freaking on the inside. I just knew that I was fixing to get stabbed. Only thing I could think to do was "Hit first and hurt them as quick as I can." I pulled my pocket knocker out and started flailing them with it. After the first two dropped I was so adrenalized I couldn't stop myself and went after the other three. I took some pretty good hits and gave everyone of them a reason to remember me. All I could think was either hurt them or I would never see my kids again. Scared me pretty bad but I came out alive.

In a follow-up comment, he said this:

I really think that not seeing my kids made me take off any restraints I might have had. I always tried to talk a situation down; I wasn't being paid to start trouble. This was a time that talking meant I was weak and scared in their eyes. I couldn't afford to let that happen. I don't espouse violence as a solution to problems but it sometime is your only option. I didn't know what these guys were planning or carrying so I had to do anything I could to go home.

Fighting for something other than yourself is perhaps one of the most powerful ways to defeat negative thoughts. When you have more to live for than your own life, things change on a fundamental level.

Here's how I see it:

I have two kids and a kind lady I love very much. I want to grow old with her and see my kids grow up into adulthood and hopefully teach my grandkids how to kick the schoolyard bully's ass. Every day when I go out, I want to come back home to them. I don't want to go to jail, nor do I really want to hurt anybody else. But I want to end up dead even less. I have responsibilities toward them as a father and a partner. I **have to** make it back in one piece, no matter what.

Looking at it that way, if negative thoughts do come up, you have another image to replace them with: getting to spend more time with your loved ones. All you have to do to achieve that result is **fight your way out of the bad situation you're in and get home in one piece.** *Despite all the fear you might feel or the thoughts undermining your determination,* that's your ultimate goal.

173

Guest Posts

Over the years, I've had the good fortune and the pleasure to meet a lot of fellow authors and martial artists. Because I like their books and videos, I want to make sure you know about them too. Which is why I review their products on my blog but also why I do the occasional guest post there. Usually, I get a ton of positive feedback on those posts from my readers.

That's why I asked several of my friends to write something for this book: so you can get a sample of what they have to offer. Hopefully, you'll like it well enough to check out their books and videos.

I also wrote a short note at the beginning of each guest post to introduce them. But also to give some feedback and point out certain things I feel are important.

Finally, I didn't give these writers any detailed instructions on what to write about or how to do so. I only explained the nature of my blog, the purpose of this book and then gave them all the freedom they needed to write whatever they wanted. I hope you'll like what they came up with.

I know I did.

"Be open to Learning" by Loren W. Christensen

Note: Loren sent me this after reading my post on "Unusual places to train and teach." An empty Saigon street during the Vietnam War certainly qualifies as "unusual"! Enjoy his guest post.

I was a brown belt when I went to Vietnam in 1969 as a Military Policeman. Many Vietnamese soldiers as well as Korean soldiers wore small, black squares above their green fatigue shirt pockets denoting how many black belts they had earned. Those with two rows had earned belts in two fighting arts.

Some of the ROK (Republic of Korea) Marines had three rows of black squares, anywhere from three to five squares in each row. Often, the more black squares a soldier had, the more chiseled his features and the harder his physique.

On one occasion, early into my tour, I was assigned to guard a building on an empty Saigon street at 2a.m. (curfew was at 1a.m.) with a rather dignified South Vietnamese military policeman who had two rows, three black squares in each, over his fatigue shirt pocket. To break the ice, I indicated that I had also trained in the martial arts, at which his face brightened and he pointed to the squares on his shirt. For the next several hours, my new friend and I swapped techniques, mostly by pantomime, and with what little English he knew and what Vietnamese I had learned.

At one point, he stepped over to a traffic sign that was attached to a tree about a foot above my six-foot-high head. He looked at it for a moment, then spun like a top, his kicking leg shooting out before it hooked back to slam that sign with the heel of what had been his rear foot, a foot wearing a heavy combat boot. I remember jumping back, probably with my mouth hanging open, going, "What was that?"

Although at that time I had been training in the martial arts for four years, I had never been taught the spinning hook kick. I had learned the spinning straight back kick, but not the spinning hook. I didn't even know it existed at that time until I saw my Vietnamese soldier friend nearly rip that high sign from the tree.

So for the next couple of hours he taught me the kick. We leaned our M-16s against the tree, stripped off our flak vests, pistol belts and shirts, and commenced to train. He was most patient with me as I stumbled about, but by the end of our session, I have to say that I could do a pretty good spinning hook. Of course kicking as high as that sign was a ways in the future, but that night I could hit the trunk like a bandit.

The point of this story is to recognize that you can learn from anyone, anywhere. Over the years, I've learned from white belts, from things non-martial artists have asked me, from the school of hard knocks on the street, and once, many years ago, from a Vietnamese soldier on a sticky-hot, Saigon night, as artillery rumbled in the distance and shook the windows of nearby buildings.

You learn something every day if you pay attention. ~Ray LeBlond

Learning is a treasure that will follow its owner everywhere. ~Chinese Proverb

You can reach Loren at his site: www.lwcbooks.com

"MMA and self defense" by Mark Mireles

Note: This is a guest post by a fellow author and amazing fighter, Mark Mireles. If you are into MMA and you got a bit upset after reading some of my writing on this sport, please read this guest post carefully. Mark has both extensive knowledge in MMA, as well as tons of experience as a decorated LAPD officer. He knows both the Octagon and the street, which makes him well placed to comment on them both.

The Ultimate Martial Arts Question – Which Came First the Chicken or the Egg?

I'm a Wim's Blog reader. I don't say much on the blog but I read and reflect. It has been said "observe much, learn much, train much". Sage advice. In my voyaging time, I had the opportunity to follow the thread that outlined the argument between self defense, martial arts training and mixed martial arts.

The discussion was that no matter how visceral and brutal MMA is at the end of the day, it's a sport that is governed by rules. There were several posts that interjected the fact that MMA does not include weapons defenses and multiple attackers. These are good points indeed. Although the self-defense crowd was very professional, at the end MMA was viewed as sport.

The MMA crowd argued that MMA was an effective fighting system because it arose out of the traditional martial arts. MMA was deemed a modern fighting system that was a sport but could be effectively used as a practical form of hand-to-hand combat. The sum was greater than its parts. Transversely, the traditional form of martial arts was viewed as limited because it didn't address all ranges of real fighting.

At the end of the day, it appeared that the two groups agreed to disagree agreeably. From my computer (being a voyeur) I thought

177

both sides made solid points and it got me thinking. Contemplating the point of view of both camps, I had the opportunity to witness something and wanted to share it with the "Wim-ers" (yes I just coined us, Wim's Blog enthusiasts). If you don't know me or my books let me tell you were I'm coming from.

Wim did an interview with me some time ago. If you didn't read it, let me introduce myself. I've been a street cop for over 20 years and been practicing martial arts since 1977. After years of street experience and martial arts training, I came to my own conclusions related to real fighting, training, and teaching.

The one thing that I learned for sure is that people have to come to their own reality. Reality is always best when it's based on experience. I also learned that I never really teach my art, I share it with others. After all, I can never fight like someone else and no one will ever fight just like me. So I share my experience and base it on concepts that are pretty universal. I don't know it all but I have observed much, learned much, trained much.

Being a cop, I've had to subdue some of the most violent predators that the human mammal has to offer: the ones that when they came into the world should have had a disclaimer stamped of their foreheads "Defective Product." In short, I'll tell you that I came from combative sports and had to take what I learned and make adjustments to make what I knew was street effective. I do mixed martial arts for the purpose of self-preservation and I'm a big fan of the UFC and MMA. I do and like both. Yes, it can be done although it's not for everyone.

I'll get to the story here soon, but I want to take a moment to share what I was thinking about the MMA vs. Self Defense thread because, like I said, I do and like both. I saw validity in both sides but the one thing that stuck out in my mind was that it's not the system, but it's who's doing the fighting.

It is the individual aspect, the mental aspect, and ultimately what is in the soul of the individual at the moment of truth. In the moment of truth for the person with the killer instinct, or, what Marc "Animal"

MacYoung has called the Proper Combat Attitude or "PCA", -karate, judo, or MMA, or a set of keys in the hands of an old lady – It's the right person with the right attitude, a place where opportunity meets preparation. Again, the personal factor is the x-factor. It's not the system – it's who's doing the fighting. All systems are artificial. The individual that makes the art work or not work.

So here's the story. I work at night primarily. When the sun goes down the criminal element is waking up, reading the newspaper, and pondering what capers they will pull while enjoying their nocturnal morning coffee (or hitting the meth pipe with a bowl of cereal). A few nights ago, a couple of gangbangers had finished their power breakfast, kissed the wives goodbye, and headed to the office. There business was armed robbery.

The protagonist of our story is a male college student who we will call "Johnny". Johnny was studying late and decided that he was in need of more caffeine so he headed to the corner market to get an energy drink with caffeine galore. Our two villains had acquired business intel that people who go to the store at night usually have money in their pocket and they engage in negotiations, with gun in hand. Of course, a hostile takeover is always a part of their business plan.

While Johnny was thinking about his upcoming algebra test, the gangsters walked up to him outside the market and demanded his money or his life. Johnny later told us that he was shocked and scared but when he saw the gun he knew he was going to have to act in self-defense. As Johnny told it, the crooks said, "Give us your money" and then one of the bad guys pulled his shirt up and exposed the butt of a gun and said "give it up now." So Johnny gave it up in the form of a major league ass whipping that left some of the worst injuries inflicted I've ever seen.

Our villains were handling their business, but did not realize they just weren't very good at it. On the night in question, the bad guys theorized that if they got caught with a real gun, they would be screwed, so they took a tequila bottle shaped as a pistol. They went so far as to spray paint it black to make it look like a real gun. Certainly, if they had a real gun, no one would be stupid enough to object to two of them beefing up their corporate account. Bad idea, but we are not dealing with rocket scientists here.

The wild card (the x-factor) in all of this was Johnny. In the moment of fight or flight, Johnny decided to fight. And so he fought. Johnny said he thought the gangster with the gun was going to shoot him. Johnny first pinned the gun down in the bad guy's waistband and then punched him in the face so hard it made bad guy number two do a step back. According to a witness, it sounded like a baseball bat hitting a watermelon. Johnny then ripped the gun away out of the gangster's waistband and began to beat his face in with it.

Made of glass, the "gun" exploded on impact of the bad guys face creating a cornucopia of glass fragments and chips of black spray paint which soon disappeared behind a sea of red blood. But Johnny was no ordinary student. Johnny was doing what all the kids are doing today: mixed martial arts and he was doing it for fun.

A year before Johnny wanted to do something different so he went to gym to learn kick boxing and then began to work in other classes and before he knew it he was training in mixed martial arts. He wasn't a professional fighter and he wasn't a reality based self-defense practitioner either. He was a kid learning to fight and I'm not even sure he knew what that training and exposure to the arts really meant.

When we (the cops) caught up to the fleeing enterprisers in the getaway car, bad guy one was covered in blood. He had sustained several deep wounds that would take painful months to heal. As he alighted from the car, he crawled and collapsed. He then vomited excretion that could not be mistaken for anything than larva that can only result from a head injury.

After trying to convince us that they were both victims of an attack, the true story was pieced together thanks to numerous 9-1-1 calls from witnesses. It was a major league ass kicking on a criminal, a robbery that went bad.

The only moral to this didactic story is that crime doesn't pay. What I got out of it was that a mixed martial artist that has practiced purely for sport, for fun, had defended himself and even preformed a gun takeaway. It reinforced what I had come to learn a long time ago: it's not the system, it's who's doing the fighting or put another way not the size of the dog in the fight – it's the size of the fight in the dog. Now I'm going back to voyaging.

Guest Post by Kris Wilder

Note: Kris's guest post is short but sweet. It's also un-complicated, which is his whole point. However, as *complicated* is not the same thing as *difficult*, *simple* is not the same thing as *easy*. Sometimes, it's good to be reminded of that.

Listening to the radio the other day I heard the show host say that one of his professors at Hillsdale College complained to the students that their papers were full of fluff, that the students spent too much effort in just filling the mandated number of pages. For example, if students were told, "Your assignment this week is to write a five-page paper on....", their response would be to simply fill up five pages. The professor, in an effort to demonstrate his point that many of the words written by the students were meaningless and didn't add value, decided to have them write a one-page paper. The show host then went on about how difficult it was to write that paper. Paragraph, phrase and each word had to succinctly convey the core issues of the topic.

The human mind loves complexity, but is it really necessary? Now understand that I make distinction between complexity and diversity. Look at it this way: nature builds diversity from a series of simple commands. In fact, what appears to be complex is really just a compounding of simple commands.

As you may already know from reading other posts, I am not the biggest fan of complexity, and especially in the martial arts, because I am sure that much of it is just machinations designed to titillate the mind like a shiny fishing lure to a trout.

Frankly, simplicity and efficiency go hand-in-hand (see nature once again) and I am not inclined to back off from that position. Complexity breaks down, and I don't need a fragile martial arts technique, I need a simple, vigorous, dependable, go-to technique.

Now here is proof of that from the world of martial arts. Don't forget that world-famous judo champion Yasuhiro Yamashita was famous for using o soto gari, one of the first learned and most basic throws of Judo, to win:

'85 All-Japan Championships – Tokyo, Japan
'84 Olympic Games (Open) – Los Angeles, CA, USA
'84 All-Japan Championships – Tokyo, Japan
'83 World Championships (+95kg) – Moscow, Russia
'83 All-Japan Championships – Tokyo, Japan
'82 All-Japan Championships – Tokyo, Japan
'81 World Championships (+95kg & Open) – Maastricht, Holland
'81 All-Japan Championships – Tokyo, Japan
'80 All-Japan Championships – Tokyo, Japan
'79 World Championships (+95kg) – Paris, France
'79 All-Japan Championships – Tokyo, Japan
'78 All-Japan Championships – Tokyo, Japan
'77 All-Japan Championships – Tokyo, Japan

Thanks to Neil Ohlenkamp for the list of championships.

You can reach Kris at his site: www.westseattlekarate.com

"Three keys to joint lock success" by Alain Burrese

Note: Though I started out in ju-jitsu, I was never a big fan of joint locks. It preferred striking techniques over turning people into pretzels. As I got older though (and better at it), joint locks made more sense to me. Alain's three keys are spot on in my opinion. Had my teachers explained them to me when I started learning the locks as a teenager, I might have liked them a whole lot better.

Many people engage in the debate of whether joint locks work in real life situations. I even see them about the video clips from my DVDs on YouTube. I try to stay out of the non-constructive exchanges because I find it a waste of time to engage in flame wars on the Internet with people you don't even know. I know joint locks work, I've used them. I also know people who have used them in real encounters, so I don't need to prove to anyone that they work. I will say this though; I have not used "all" of the joint locks that I teach in actual situations. Considering the size of the Hapkido curriculum, you'd have to fight quite a bit to use everything.

I've also been in altercations and fights where I didn't even think of using joint locks, but resorted to other techniques such as striking, kicking, kneeing, and anything else that kept me from being harmed until I could disengage from the fight. And yes, that sometimes meant me up, him down and hurt, and me getting out of the area as fast as I could. However, that does not negate the fact that joint locks are valid and useful techniques for certain circumstances. I've used them successfully to escort people outside when working security and I've used them for other situations that did not warrant knocking a person's head off with a strike or smashing a knee cap with a kick. Not every physical encounter entails you going up against a three hundred pound steroid raged monster. There are many situations where a small amount of physical persuasion, which joint locks and pressure points are good for, is all that's needed to safely end the situation.

I also must point out that I like joint locks, and that is one of the reasons Hapkido is my primary art and that I teach many locks through seminars and DVDs, as well as other Hapkido techniques and self-defense principles. I enjoy learning how the body works, and how to execute locks in the most efficient manner, using my strengths against an opponent's weaknesses. I know that there is no technique which is perfect for all situations, and I know that joint locks take more time to learn and become proficient at than basic striking and kicking. However, once mastered, joint locking techniques allow you to control or subdue an opponent without injuring them, or if justified, you can cause severe and permanent damage. It is for all of these reasons, as well as others, that I continue to learn, perfect, and teach joint locks. To help with your learning and training, here are three keys I've found to assist you with making joint locks work.

Surprise

If a person knows what you are going to do, it is much easier to defend against. If I tell you I'm going to execute a wrist lock, you will pull your hand away and not let me apply the lock. I'm certainly not going to verbally tell a person what I'm going to do, but many people "tell" their opponent just that by telegraphing their techniques. Therefore, it is important to not let your opponent know what you are up to until it is too late. Once a lock is locked on correctly, there is often little a person can do to get loose. So don't let them defeat your technique in its early stages, surprise them with it.

Speed

Part of surprise is found in speed. You must be able to quickly execute a locking technique. If you perform it slowly, the person will figure out what you are doing and may be able to pull the limb you are trying to lock from your grasp before the technique is locked on properly. If you are moving too slow, your opponent may be able to execute his technique against you before the lock is locked on. If his technique happens to be a palm heel to your face, you may be standing there with watering eyes and a broken nose wondering why your lock failed. It may not be that the lock failed, but you failed to execute it before getting smashed in the face.

Proper Technique

You can be fast and catch your opponent by surprise and still have a lock fail if you don't execute it correctly with proper technique. Locks require correct angles and specific application to maximize their effectiveness. If your angle is off, if you are not applying pressure in the correct place or in the proper manner, or if you are not using your body weight and motion to enhance the effectiveness of your technique, your lock may fail. I encourage everyone to analyze techniques and why they work, as well as body motion and weight transfer to ensure the economy of motion and correct application of technique is performed. Remember, to be effective with your locking techniques, you must be fast, smooth and skillful, and to reach this level requires a lot of practice.

It is extremely important to combine all the proper ingredients when executing joint locks. This is why I spend time teaching these concepts, and emphasize them, sometimes repetitively, to everyone I instruct. Joint locks work in certain situations. You won't force a technique, but rather use it when the opportunity arises. By learning, practicing, and understanding locks to the point you can execute them with surprise, speed, and proper technique, you'll have additional tools in your tool box for those situations when locking a person up is the best choice of action.

Alain Burrese is the author of Hard-Won Wisdom From The School of Hard Knocks, Hapkido Hoshinsul, Streetfighting Essentials, Hapkido Cane, and the Lock On: Joint Locking Essentials series. He teaches seminars on joint locks, self-defense, safety, and the Hapkido cane. Additionally, he teaches how to live with the Warrior's Edge. He can be reached though his websites www.yourwarriorsedge.com and www.burrese.com

Guest Post by Rory Miller

Note: In this post, Rory touches upon a critical issue for practitioners of the arts: it's "Martial" arts. As in: "Mars, god of war." You can definitely train for other goals such as health or fun, but in origin, what you're practicing is how to kill, injure and maim people. The moment you forget that or refuse to accept it, that's when you start veering off the path and are heading into LaLa-land.

Note how I didn't say you have to go out and kill people, not at all. But you have to accept the purpose of the art you're practicing, however uncomfortable that makes you. If you don't want to do that, maybe you should pick up aerobics. There's no shame in that.

Sometimes I get a disconnect with martial artists. I train because occasionally, either to keep the peace or to get home, I need to stop bad people from doing bad things. If and when I need to break a human being, I want to do it as efficiently as possible.

Maximum speed, efficiency and effect. And maximum safety, too. If I get hurt today I'll be less safe tomorrow.

It makes some stuff very clear: I train because I want to go home and hug my wife, every night. To do that, I need to be very good at breaking people.

Martial arts, at its core, is the science of breaking people. The art of manufacturing cripples and corpses. You can pretty it up, I suppose, but I don't think you can do so and be truly mindful. An elegant kick is a marvel of athletic prowess; a good throw is the perfect expression of applied physics. They are also shattering ribs and snapping necks.

It is not an either/or. If you practice martial arts, no matter how beautiful or gentle, the purpose was originally pretty ugly and brutal. The true meaning and intent of each action is destruction.

187

You can pretend it isn't. Whatever you need to say so that you can sleep at night. Talk harmony and peace. But it originated from harm and pieces. Even if you have lost sight of that, or choose to live in denial, some of us haven't. Some of us can't.

There is an exception. Sports martial arts are pure. The rules that define what they are doing and what they are training for are one and the same. (I'd personally like a little more emphasis on sportsmanship, but that's an artifact of my generation.) Some practitioners think they are doing more than they are… but at the very least they are not practicing knocking someone out and pretending it is an expression of a peaceful soul. They aren't, and can't afford to be, that deluded.

We raise some of our own food. That means that we slaughter our chickens or goats for meat. We kill them, quickly, efficiently and humanely. This is how I was taught and how I taught my children.

How weird it would be to sit with someone on a bus who strikes up a conversation, "I slaughter chickens for a hobby. Been doing it for years. I'm really good at it."

Let's say, for just a moment, that you don't pretend not to hear or look for another seat. That you, yourself, live on a farm and have killed a few chickens. "Really," you say, "as a hobby? You must have a friend who has a farm or something."

"Oh, no, " the chicken-killing hobbyist says, "I go to classes three times a week. I've been going for five years. I'll be ready to open my own school soon."

Wow, because you had no idea people went to classes to slaughter chickens. That's a chore you did everything you could to get out of. Some people find it fun? Some people pay to do it? "Where do you do this?" you ask, "How many chickens do you slaughter a week?"

He laughs, "I do it at a nice gym down town. We don't actually kill anything, we just practice the techniques. Some of our techniques have been handed down unchanged for two hundred years. Some are secrets that take years to understand. If I keep training, I'll get my master chicken killing certificate in a few years."

Makes you think, doesn't it? As weird as killing chickens is as a hobby, pretending to kill chickens? Seriously?

You can reach Rory at: www.chirontraining.com

Guest post by Marc "Animal" MacYoung

Note: Marc nails it on another one of those crucial topics martial artists need to ingrain in everything they do: no matter how much you want to hit somebody fifteen times and then re-stomp his groin, that doesn't make it self-defense. Even if the guy started trouble to begin with and he most certainly deserves it, you still can't go ape-shit on him **and** call it self-defense. Call it something else. Call it "a fight" or "an ass-whooping" but not self-defense.

I know this might bother a lot of people but in this post, Marc pops a couple bubbles some readers might not want him to touch. Because the implications reach far and wide; they touch everything you do in your art. It's OK if you disagree with him, but at the very least give it some thought and then go talk to a lawyer who actually tries self-defense cases. You might be surprised...

Before we start -- if you can -- give me the clinical definition of insanity.

Okay, so that's a trick question. There is no such thing. There are, however, hundreds, if not thousands, of terms used by psychologists, health care workers and medical professionals to identify particular types of mental illness and problems.

Yet, everyone 'knows' what insanity is. It's a generalized, popular term. A term, if you say it, the average person 'knows' what you're talking about. Right?

Well, no. It's too broad, it's too vague, and it's pretty much a blanket term that means 'whatever someone wants it to mean,' – with special emphasis on stupid and something you disagree with.

Insanity is, however, a legal term. In fact, here's a quick run down:

A person is insane, and is not responsible for criminal conduct, if, at the time of such conduct, as a result of a severe mental disease or defect, he was unable to appreciate the nature and quality or the wrongfulness of his acts.

This is because willful intent is an essential part of most offenses; and a person who is insane is not capable of forming such intent. Mental disease or defect does not otherwise constitute a defense; the person has the burden of proving the defense of insanity by clear and convincing evidence.

From a legal standpoint, they don't care if you are schizophrenic, bipolar, addicted or suffer from an antisocial personality disorder (those are specific psychological issues). The big question in the legal context is 'Did you know it was wrong when you did it?' And knowing that, you did it anyway. (For example: killing someone by running him or her over because you were enraged is an intentional act of malice with full knowledge and understanding of what you did. Contrast this against the woman, who killed another driver in a T-bone 'accident,' because she was trying to escape from the busload of angels chasing her. One goes to prison, one goes to the psych ward.)

My point is, while everyone uses the term' insanity,' the closest thing you get to a professional definition is legal.

The same thing applies to the term 'self-defense.'

Even though everyone and his or her brother knows what it means (and a lot of people pay for 'self-defense training'), in the final analysis self-defense is a legal term.

More than that, there are some very strict definitions involved that **you** must tailor your actions to meet. Definitions, if your actions don't conform to them, then determine what you did wasn't self-defense. No matter how much you tell yourself they were.

This becomes particularly important because self-defense is an 'affirmative defense.' When you claim, 'self-defense,' you are confessing to an action that is normally a crime!

By claiming 'self-defense,' you've just done the majority of the prosecution's job of putting you in the prison showers. Not a smart move if it wasn't. And this is where not knowing what self-defense really is and isn't comes back and bites you in the butt.

From a legal standpoint, fighting is deemed 'mutual assault,' 'consensual combat' or however they say it where you are. The underlying issue in any of those is: If you are 'fighting,' you are part of the problem.

That means, no matter how much you tell yourself "He started it!", **if** you are deemed to be fighting, then you are viewed as a willing participant in illegal violence. What you did and said is going to be closely examined. Even if he threw the first punch, you mentioning his testicles on his mother's chin – which seemed like such a good idea at the time – is going to be used against you. Your comments about his mother's sexual proclivities is viewed – both legally and socially -- as you participating in the creation, escalation and execution of violence.

That's because you didn't have to say it. In fact, you had the option to leave, apologize and calm things down, instead you decided to attack with words and later, retaliate with fists.

That last point is what screws up most people's claim of 'self-defense.' It's also one of those, 'it seemed like a good idea at the time' issues. Unfortunately when you are adrenalized and have just been hit, it is extremely easy to self-justify a retaliatory attack as self-defense.

To understand this, you have to understand how violence usually occurs. While all out, blitzkrieg assaults do occasionally happen, a majority of violence looks like this: two people in conflict, yelling, screaming, threat displays, etc. One person steps up, strikes, steps back and then continues yelling to make his point. From here it can go several ways. The person who was struck can:

a) Submit
b) Dance back and start yelling louder
c) Physically retaliate
d) Others intervene and break it up.

It is point C that interests us in the context of self-defense. Pay special attention to the facts that

a) The aggressor is no longer physically attacking
b) There is a distance between the two parties.

Here is where adrenaline will get you into trouble. Under these circumstances it is easy to believe you are still under attack -- so you react according to that perception. Another version is that you want to 'even the score.' Makes sense right?

Congratulations, you've just left self-defense and stepped into 'willing participation' and illegal assault.

What the security video is going to show is you were hit and then, either you or the other person moved out of attack range. Then it's going to show you stepping close again and throwing a retaliatory strike. No matter what your little adrenalized monkey brain is telling you, this is NOT self-defense. It is an act of participation and retaliation.

If these were your actions, then the **last** thing you want to do is claim 'self-defense.' Yes, he committed an illegal assault on you. By counter assaulting him when he was not in the process of attacking you again, you too have committed an illegal assault.

And by claiming 'self-defense' you've just confessed to that crime.

Self-defense means you – literally – have no choice about being in a violent situation. For example, you're walking out of a train station and you are unexpectedly jumped by a pack of hooligans or attacked by an individual.

A key element here is: What your goals are. Both for your physical safety and whether or not you will be arrested. If you are fighting your goal is usually to 'win' --with additional caveats of teaching someone a lesson, revenge, even the score and lots of other stuff. The problem with these goals is they often result in people sticking around and working towards achieving them. In case you missed it, that's known as fighting and is illegal.

Your self-defense goal is to stop the threat as soon as possible.

A key element of violence is you have to be there in order for it to happen. People don't realize the importance of this concept, but if you aren't there, it's not happening now is it? This teaches us an important lesson: **if** you can't get out of there earlier (and that's a big 'if'), then, when you have to go physical, your goal is not to win. Instead, fight to get out of there!

If I try to stay to 'win,' or I believe I have to stand there and hit him sixteen times before I can 'safely' get away, odds are good something will go wrong. Not only will I be more likely to get hurt, but the video is going to show me standing there fighting. No matter what I 'thought' I was doing, that's how the police, judge and jury are going to see it.

On the other hand, someone attacks, I block and drill him a good one **as** I'm getting out of there, that's a lot more defensible in the eyes of the law as 'self-defense' than me trying to 'win.'

Keep this self-defense goal in mind as you train for self-defense. That's because training to fight and calling it self-defense will get you into some deep kim chee.

You can reach Marc at: www.nononsenseselfdefense.com

Author's note

While writing this book, I came across all those posts I had written years ago for my blog and worked on them again. This turned out to be a lot more fun than I expected, which is saying something because I usually hate editing and rewrites. I also noticed certain themes coming back, which helped me highlight certain parts a bit more and get rid of some of the clutter. I hope this improved the writing and therefore your enjoyment while reading this book.

This was also an opportunity to work with some of my friends by asking them for a contribution. In most of my projects, that just isn't possible so it was a blast to do so here and I plan on doing this again in the following volumes. I think their pieces make a fine addition to mine and I hope you enjoyed them as much as I did.

If you did and you like this book, there is something you can do to help me out: spread the word.

Write a review wherever you bought this book (on Amazon or elsewhere), on your blog or in an internet forum. Tell your friends about it via email, Facebook, Twitter or any other way you might think of. Even if it's just a line or two, it would make all the difference in the world to me and be very much appreciated

Also, feel free to get in touch with me and tell me which parts you liked best. Or the ones you didn't like at all. With your feedback I can make sure the following books are tailored more to what you, the reader, want to see. You can reach me here:

My site: www.wimdemeere.com
My blog, I'm pretty active there: www.wimsblog.com
Facebook: www.facebook.com/WimDemeerePage
Twitter: www.twitter.com/wimdemeere
Thank you for your support!

About the Author

Wim Demeere began training at the age of 14, studying the grappling arts of judo and jujitsu for several years before turning to the kick/punch arts of traditional kung fu and full-contact fighting. Over the years he has studied a broad range of other fighting styles, including muay Thai, kali, pentjak silat and shootfighting. Since the late 1990s, he has been studying tai chi chuan and its martial applications.

Wim's competitive years saw him win four national titles and a bronze medal at the 1995 World Wushu Championships. In 2001, he became the national coach of the Belgian Wushu fighting team. A full-time personal trainer in his native country of Belgium, Wim instructs both business executives and athletes in nutrition, strength and endurance, and a variety of martial arts styles. He has managed a corporate wellness center and regularly gives lectures and workshops in the corporate world.

You can contact Wim through his website www.wimdemeere.com and at his blog www.wimsblog.com.

Printed in Great Britain
by Amazon